T0214651

Lecture Notes in Computer Science   11911

More information about this series at http://www.springer.com/series/7409

Meikang Qiu (Ed.)

Smart Blockchain

Second International Conference, SmartBlock 2019
Birmingham, UK, October 11–13, 2019
Proceedings

 Springer

Editor
Meikang Qiu
Columbia University
New York, NY, USA

ISSN 0302-9743   ISSN 1611-3349   (electronic)
Lecture Notes in Computer Science
ISBN 978-3-030-34082-7   ISBN 978-3-030-34083-4   (eBook)
https://doi.org/10.1007/978-3-030-34083-4

LNCS Sublibrary: SL3 – Information Systems and Applications, incl. Internet/Web, and HCI

This Springer imprint is published by the registered company Springer Nature Switzerland AG
The registered company address is: Gewerbestrasse 11, 6330 Cham, Switzerland

Preface

This volume contains the papers presented at SmartBlock 2019: The Second International conference on SmartBlock held during October 11–13, 2019, in Birmingham, UK.

There were 100 submissions. Each submission was reviewed by at least three, and on average four, Program Committee members. The committee decided to accept 13 papers.

The recent rapid development of blockchain has attracted major attention from both academia and industry. Migrating centralized computing to decentralized computing seems to be the main stream method in establishing a trusted and secure storage and trading environment. However, it is too early to make a solid statement about the adoption of blockchain technology, since there are many unsolved problems in the field. The success of blockchain technique in Bit-coin does not mean the technique can be successfully deployed in all domains. This international conference aims to gather the most up-to-date papers in the field of blockchain and provides a platform for both scholars and practitioners.

The scope of SmartBlock covers a broad range of topics related to blockchain realms, from privacy-preserving solutions to designing advanced blockchain mechanism, from empirical studies to practical manuals. All high-quality current work is highly welcomed!

SmartBlock 2019 was organized by the SmartBlock 2019 committees. We warmly thank the conference sponsors: Springer LNCS, Birmingham City University, Columbia University, Beijing Institute of Technology, North America Chinese Talents Association, and Longxiang High Tech Group Inc.

September 2019   Meikang Qiu

Organization

General Chairs

Meikang Qiu	Columbia University, USA
Mark Sharma	Birmingham City University, UK

Program Chairs

Yonghao Wang	Birmingham City University, UK
Liehuang Zhu	Beijing Institute of Technology, China
Gerard Memmi	Télécom ParisTech, France

Local Chairs

Xiangyu Gao	New York University, USA
Paul Kearney	Birmingham City University, UK

Publicity Chairs

Hui Zhao	Henan University, China
Han Qiu	Télécom ParisTech, France
Zhenyu Guan	Beihang University, China

Technical Committee

Jeremy Foss	Birmingham City University, UK
Cham Athwal	Birmingham City University, UK
Andrew Aftelak	Birmingham City University, UK
Yue Hu	Louisiana State University, USA
Aniello Castiglione	University of Salerno, Italy
Maribel Fernandez	King's College, University of London, UK
Hao Hu	Nanjing University, China
Oluwaseyi Oginni	Birmingham City University, UK
Alan Dolhasz	Birmingham City University, UK
Thomas Austin	San Jose State University, USA
Aniello Castiglione	University of Salerno, Italy
Zhiyuan Tan	Edinburgh Napier University, UK
William Campbell	Birmingham City University, UK
Xiang He	Birmingham City University, UK
Mohammad Patwary	Birmingham City University, UK
Peter Bull	QA Ltd, UK
Hendri Murfi	Universitas Indonesia, Indonesia

Zengpeng Li	Lancaster University, UK
Wenbo Shi	Inha University, South Korea
Pietro Ferrara	JuliaSoft SRL, Italy
Ke Miao	Mitacs Inc., Canada
Dalia El B. Abdelghany Ashmawy	Birmingham City University, UK
Xiaohu Zhou	Birmingham City University, UK
Guangxia Xu	Chongqing University of Posts and Telecomunications, China
Kui Zhang	Birmingham City University, UK
Vitor Jesus	Birmingham City University, UK
Matthew Roach	Swansea University, UK
Chunhua Deng	Wuhan University of Science and Technology, China
Katie Cover	Pennsylvania State University, USA
Shishank Shishank	Birmingham City University, UK
Jinguang Gu	Wuhan University of Science and Technology, China
Wei Cai	Chinese University of Hong Kong, Hong Kong, China
Junwei Zhang	Xidian University, China
Jue Wang	SCCAS, China
Hao Tang	City University of New York, USA
Md Ali	Rider University, USA
Paul Kearney	Birmingham City University, UK
Li Bo	Beihang University, China
Zijian Zhang	Beijing Institute of Technology, China
Meng Ma	Peking University, China
Cheng Zhang	Waseda University, Japan
Fausto Spoto	University of Verona, Italy
Song Yang	Beijing Institute of Technology, China
Lixin Tao	Pace University, USA
Rehan Bhana	Birmingham City University, UK
Ian A. Williams	CEBE, Birmingham City University, UK
Shaojing Fu	National University of Defense Technology, China
Agostino Cortesi	Università Ca' Foscari, Italy
Yunxia Liu	Huazhong University of Science and Technology, China
Yongxin Zhu	Chinese Academy of Sciences, China
Songmao Zhang	Chinese Academy of Sciences, China
Jongpil Jeong	Sungkyunkwan University, South Korea
Ding Wang	Peking University, China
Wenjia Li	New York Institute of Technology, USA
Peng Zhang	Stony Brook University, USA
Jeroen van den Bos	Netherlands Forensic Institute, The Netherlands
Ron Austin	Birmingham City University, UK
Wayne Collymore	Birmingham City University, UK

Haibo Zhang   University of Otago, New Zealand
Suman Kumar   Troy University, USA
Shui Yu   Deakin University, Australia
Emmanuel Bernardez   IBM Research, USA

Contents

Research on Privacy Protection in IoT System Based on Blockchain

Shiping Fan[1], Liang Song[1(✉)], and Chunyan Sang[2]

[1] School of Communication and Information Engineering, Chongqing University of Posts and Telecommunications, Chongqing 400065, China
fansp@cqupt.edu.cn, songliang159@gmail.com
[2] School of Software Engineering, Chongqing University of Posts and Telecommunications, Chongqing 400065, China
sangcy@cqupt.edu.cn

Abstract. The Internet of Things (IoT) is an important area of next-generation information technology, and its value and significance are widely recognized. While providing development opportunities, the IoT also presents major challenges. Security and privacy have become severe issues that cannot be ignored in the development of the IoT in this paper, so we will propose an IoT information security protection scheme based on blockchain technology. The scheme utilizes the security features of the blockchain combined with the AES encryption algorithm to encrypt the original IoT information, and the ciphertext distributed storage can effectively solve the IoT data storage problem. Experiments shown in this scheme could reduce the operation and credit cost of centralized network. At the same time, the blockchain-based IoT information security protection scheme combined with cryptography knowledge can effectively solved the big data management and trust faced in the development of the IoT, security and privacy issues.

Keywords: Blockchain · IoT information security · IoT data storage · IPFS · Access control

This work is supported by the National Natural Science Foundation (Grant No. 61772099, 61772098); the Program for Innovation Team Building at Institutions of Higher Education in Chongqing (Grant No. CXTDG201602010); Chongqing Science and Technology Innovation Leadership Support Program (Grant No. CSTC-CXLJRC201917); the University Outstanding Achievements Transformation Funding Project of Chongqing (Grant No. KJZH17116); the Artificial Intelligence Technology Innovation Important Subject Projects of Chongqing (cstc2017rgzn-zdyf0140); The Innovation and Entrepreneurship Demonstration Team Cultivation Plan of Chongqing (cstc2017kjrc-cxcytd0063); the Chongqing Research Program of Basic Research and Frontier Technology (Grant No. cstc2017jcyjAX0270, Grant No. cstc2018jcyjA0672, Grant No. cstc2017jcyjAX0071); the Industry Important Subject Projects of Chongqing (Grant No. CSTC2018JSZX-CYZTZX0178, Grant No. CSTC2018JSZX-CYZTZX0185).

M. Qiu (Ed.): SmartBlock 2019, LNCS 11911, pp. 1–10, 2019.
https://doi.org/10.1007/978-3-030-34083-4_1

1   Introduction

As an important field of new generation information technology, the IoT has its universal recognition of value and significance. Industrial equipment, automobiles, smart home and other items are connected to each other through the network and generating a large amount of data, combined with powerful data analysis capabilities which is expected to change the way of production and life, while generating enormous social and commercial value [1,2]. However, while the IoT providing opportunities for development, the IoT has also brought significant challenges which security and privacy have become issues that cannot be ignored in the development of the IoT [3]. The blockchain integrates technologies such as distributed data storage, peer-to-peer transmission, consensus mechanism, and encryption algorithm. It is expected to solve the weakness of IoT security, reduce the operation and credit cost of centralized network, and improve operational efficiency and industrial asset utilization. To enhance the value of the IoT system [4,5].

Blockchain is a mode for constructing and managing transaction processing through transparent and trusted rules in a peer-to-peer network environment. It has distributed peer-to-peer, chained data blocks and defenses. Typical characteristics of forgery and tamper resistance, transparency and reliability, and high reliability [6]. Gai, proposed distributed power energy trading in the peer-to-peer network environment using blockchain and transparent and credible rules to construct and manage transaction processing models [7]. Blockchain can provide two application capabilities for the IoT: one is to provide infrastructure for computing, storage, network and platform resources through peer-to-peer networks, and the other is to manage, query and analyze data in peer-to-peer networks [8]. Reference [9,10] proposed model is a distributed cloud architecture based on blockchain technology, which provides low-cost, secure, and on-demand access to the most competitive computing infrastructures in an IoT network. Zhu, proposed a controllable blockchain data management (CBDM) model that can be deployed in a cloud environment [11].

Combining the unique technical characteristics of the blockchain, this paper proposes a blockchain-based IoT information security protection scheme, which can effectively solve the problems of big data management, trust, security and privacy faced in the development of the IoT. Blockchain-based protection schemes provide trust, ownership records, transparency, and communication support for the IoT, enabling scalable device coordination, building efficient, trusted, and secure distributed IoT networks, and deploying massive amounts of devices Data-intensive applications running on the network, while providing effective protection for user privacy. In this paper, the combination of Advanced Encryption Standard (AES) algorithm and smart contract is applied to the IoT information security platform based on blockchain. The AES algorithm is used to directly process the ciphertext without divulging the real plaintext, thus ensuring the confidentiality of the data.

2 Blockchain Solves IoT Information Security Requirements

2.1 IoT Information Security Requirements

Security is the most important issue in IoT applications. The traditional IoT information security protection is protected from the IoT perceptual layer, the IoT network layer and the IoT application layer [12]. However, by controlling the availability of the network, inputting erroneous data into the network, illegally accessing personal privacy information and other means to attack the IoT system to destroy the security of the IoT, the existing security protection technology is difficult to solve [13]. In this paper, we propose the IoT and blockchain solution for IoT information security. The security requirements of the solution include: (1) data auditable and tamper-proof, (2) identity authentication, (3) privacy protection, and (4) data access control. (5) tracking violations.

2.2 Applicability of Blockchain to IoT

Blockchain classifications include public blockchain, consortium blockchain, and private blockchain [14, 15]. A comparison of each blockchain is shown in Fig. 1. Based on the requirements of the IoT, considering the large storage capacity of image, audio, video and other multi-data information content, the appropriate framework for the blockchain is to "build blocks on the internal blockchain platform and store the content itself in the external database". The scheme proposes efficient, secure authentication, privacy protection, and multi-signature-based conditional traceability methods to easily retrieve IoT data licenses, usage controls, and constraint information from the blockchain.

According to the requirements of the management of IoT data, the blockchain can only be used by authorized or multi-part administrators to manage content in a credible and tamper-proof manner, providing credible content violation traceability, and reading, writing or auditing operations must comply with access control strategy. Therefore, according to the above analysis, in this paper, we choose the consortium blockchain as the IoT information management, which is used to store the original content source for anti-counterfeiting evidence and violation of tracking, and then the content itself, content ownership, rights holder, content obligations and security requirements can be included in the consortium blockchain and authorized processing.

3 Blockchain Solves IoT Information Security

3.1 Blockchain Solution to Solve the Problem of Information Security of the IoT

This paper proposes a blockchain-based IoT information security protection scheme (IoTChain), which can effectively protect the security of IoT devices

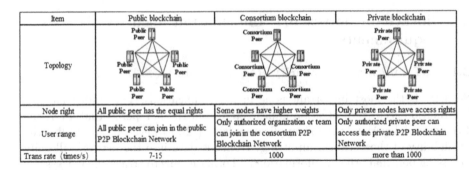

Item	Public blockchain	Consortium blockchain	Private blockchain
Topology			
Node right	All public peer has the equal rights	Some nodes have higher weights	Only private nodes have access rights
User range	All public peer can join in the public P2P Blockchain Network	Only authorized organization or team can join in the consortium P2P Blockchain Network	Only authorized private peer can access the private P2P Blockchain Network
Trans rate (times/s)	7-15	1000	more than 1000

Fig. 1. Comparison of different blockchains

to collect information, and can serve legitimate users in a correct way, providing reliable, high levels of content protection and illegal content are traceable.

In the proposed IoTChain, considering that the information storage of voice, image, video and other IoT data needs a large amount of memory, combined with the special situation of the Internet of things, we used two isolated blockchain application interfaces to store the data of the IoT. Store the original information and the original information key of IoT data respectively. By using this chain structure, the memory size problem of blockchain itself can be solved, and the access control problem can be solved by trusted authentication.

3.2   Fusion Model of Blockchain and IoT

The blockchain and IoT fusion framework proposed in this paper can be divided into four layers, from bottom to top: perception layer, network layer, blockchain layer and application layer. As shown in Fig. 2, the perceptual layer and the network layer provide the basic hardware environment and communication-related equipment facilities for the blockchain and the IoT. As an intermediate layer, the blockchain uses the hardware resources of communication and infrastructure to provide trust or consensus support mechanisms or services for IoT applications. The application layer leverages the services provided by the blockchain layer to enhance its security and privacy capabilities. The perception layer is the bottom layer of the IoT. It is the core capability to realize the perception of the IoT. It mainly solves the problem of data acquisition and connection in the biological world and the physical world [16,17]. The most commonly used radio frequency identification (RFID) technology is a non-contact automatic identification technology, which automatically recognizes target objects and acquires relevant data through radio frequency signals. The identification process does not require manual intervention and can work in each a harsh environment. RFID technology recognizes high-speed moving objects and recognizes multiple labels at the same time, making operation quick and easy.

The network layer mainly solves the problem of long-distance transmission of data obtained by the sensing layer [17]. Wireless Sensor Network (WSN) is a

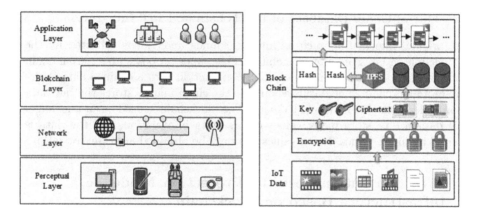

Fig. 2. Blockchain and IoT fusion model

network information system that integrates distributed information collection, information transmission and information processing technologies. It is low-cost, miniaturized, low-power and flexible. And the characteristics that are suitable for moving targets are widely valued and are important technologies related to national economic development and national security. The IoT is the ultimate perception of the entire material world through a variety of sensors and wireless sensor networks that are spread across all corners and objects.

Blockchain is a distributed network environment that constructs traceable blockchain data structures through transparent and trusted rules to implement and manage transaction processing modes. It has distributed peer-to-peer, chained data blocks and anti-counterfeiting. And typical features of three aspects: tamper resistance, transparency and reliability. The blockchain layer combines the technical characteristics of the blockchain to effectively solve the problems of big data management, trust, security and privacy faced in the development of the IoT. This layer architecture provides trust, ownership records, transparency and communication support for the IoT, enabling scalable device coordination, building an efficient, trusted, secure distributed IoT network, and deploying a massive network of devices. Data-intensive applications provide effective protection for user privacy.

The IoT application layer is a rich IoT-based application that interfaces the IoT with users, including people, organizations, and other systems. It combines with industry needs to realize the intelligent application of the IoT, and is also the fundamental goal of the development of the IoT. The industry characteristics of the IoT are mainly reflected in its application areas. At present, green agriculture, industrial monitoring, public safety, urban management, telemedicine, smart home, intelligent transportation and environmental monitoring have all tried the IoT applications.

3.3 Out-of-Chain Database of Blockchain and IoT Integration

The original information such as images, sounds and videos collected by the IoT occupies a large amount of memory. This paper proposes an external chain database for storing data information in conjunction with a chained data structure of a blockchain. The database outside the chain mainly stores the raw data information collected by the IoT device. The blockchain is used as an unchangeable database to store index values of raw data information, and the data is queried by index values. Index values can only be obtained after authorization.

4   IoT Information Security Protection Model Infrastructure Based on Blockchain

4.1 Data Storage Module

The Inter Planetary File System (IPFS) is a peer-to-peer distributed files system that seeks to connect all computing devices with the same system of files. IPFS is a network transport protocol designed to create persistent and distributed storage and shared files. IPFS is a decentralized storage network based on blockchain technology and is a content-addressable peer-to-peer hypermedia distribution protocol. The nodes in the IPFS network will form a distributed file system [18]. IPFS is a distributed file system which synthesizes successful ideas from previous peer-to-peer systems, including DHTs, BitTorrent, Git, and SFS, IPFS could even evolve the web itself [19]. Each file is uploaded to the network and is hashed and a digital fingerprint is generated. IPFS deletes files with the same hash value through the network, and compares the hash values to determine which files are redundantly duplicated, and minimizes redundant files from the root cause. When searching for a file, the hash value of the file can be used to find the file where the file is stored in the network and find the required file [20].

This paper proposes a distributed and reliable storage of IoT data information based on the combination of IPFS and encryption algorithm. It solves the problem of IoT data information storage, while considering the security and non-tampering of IoT information. The IoT information is stored in the IPFS system, and the returned hash value is encrypted to store the ciphertext in the blockchain. Authorized users can obtain the hash value of the unique index stored in the IPFS system content through the smart contract for permission verification. The user access authority is determined through the smart contract, and the flow is shown in Fig. 3. The response rule is preset in the smart contract. When the user needs to access the data information, a transaction needs to be initiated, and other nodes in the blockchain verify the transaction, and when the verification passes and the preset access rule is met, the authorization can be obtained. Obtain the key and block header data of the IoT data information, use the key decryption to obtain the index information, and obtain the original information through the index.

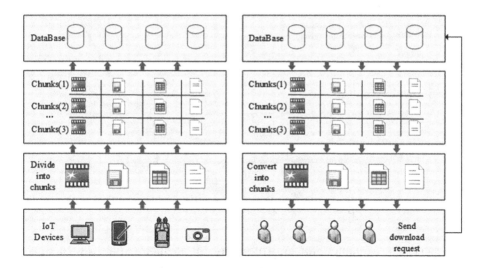

Fig. 3. IPFS file upload and download

4.2 Data Cryptographic Module

AES is a symmetric cipher that processes data in128-bit blocks. It supports key sizes of 128, 192, and 256bits and consists of 10, 12, or 14 iteration rounds, respectively. Each round mixes the data with around key, which is generated from the encryption key. Decryption inverts the iterations resulting in a partially different data path.

The cipher maintains an internal, 4-by-4 matrix of bytes, called state, on which the operations are performed. Initially state is filled with the input data block and XORed with the encryption key. Regular rounds consist of operations called sub bytes, shift rows, mix columns, and add round key. The last round bypasses mix columns [21].

Sub bytes is an invertible, nonlinear transformation. It uses 16 identical 256-byte substitution tables (S-box)for independently mapping each byte of state into another byte. S-box entries are generated by computing multiplicative in-verses in galois field $GF(2^8)$ and applying an affine trans-formation. Sub bytes can be implemented either by computing the substitution or using table lookups [22].

5 Blockchain for IoT Information Security

In this paper, we use the AES encryption algorithm, which has the advantages of simple, parallel computing, error not passing, and not easy to attack (error transmission). We performed a performance test on AES, and the test results are shown in Fig. 4. The test environment of the desktop CPU is i5-8300H 2.3 GHz memory size RAM 16 GB. From the test results, it can be seen whether AES encryption or decryption is suitable for the use of IoT information security scenarios.

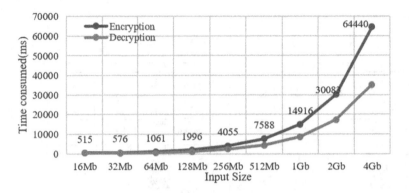

Fig. 4. AES encryption and decryption rate

In IoTChain we built a private IPFS network for information storage as a storage system for IoTChain. The simulation test results of the storage system performance of IoTChain are shown in the Fig. 5. Figure 5(a) is the delay of the node joining the public IPFS system, and Figure 5(b) is the delay of the node joining the IoTChain network. It can be seen that the average delay of the node joining the network is 1.54 ms, and the average delay of the node that can be added to the network by b is 92.96 ms, which is superior to the public network IoTChain storage system. We uploaded the data information to the IoTChain storage system, and the lena image used in this experiment was used for simulation experiments. Gets the hash value of the file returned by the IoTChain storage system. The hash value is encrypted by the AES encryption algorithm, and the encryption result is shown in Table 1. We deployed smart contracts on the Ropsten Testnet test network for performance and functional testing. The main purpose of the smart contract is to permanently store the AES encrypted ciphertext on the blockchain. The contract deployment address is shown in Table 1.

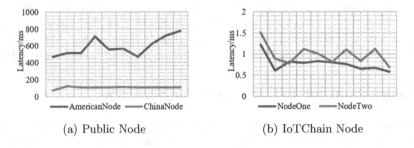

(a) Public Node   (b) IoTChain Node

Fig. 5. Delay of node joining network

Table 1. Data upload to IPFS and ciphertext upload to Blockchain

Key	Value
ImageHash in IPFS	QmaHutoUgYZF3Lepfs5wBNKHU8ij7VCAf6ho8VH38NfvMX
Key seed	w9oMoe9TYvbPb0yRfuhjKw==
Encrypted of ImageHash	NBv1TgHNsRrEIIHCItOKGxw2BuLbzG19OB33DJ7JFz7YkE2hyT9xotkR0WNgxTSA
Ethereum contract address	0xa6b4c6cf1db87fd5b2fa25118dae580248322d342bd30a61d078d3e079674853
Decrypted of ImageHash	QmaHutoUgYZF3Lepfs5wBNKHU8ij7VCAf6ho8VH38NfvMX
Transaction hash	0xc81bc1fcb8e766cea2e0f2b8c0d151118c3bc1d5d2be752895c3853685470c67
Status	Success
Block	5543565?605097 Block Confirmations
Timestamp	60 days 20 hrs ago (May-06-2019 06:49:31 AM +UTC)
From	0x7e5b7345f55797733dd13991e06d556efe67affb?
To	Contract 0x3f74edd5d2c81df73b0170f22ce7d25ef7da9191?
Input	@ NBv1TgHNsRrEIIHCItOKGxw2BuLbzG19OB33DJ7JFz7YkE2hyT9xotkR0WNgxTSA?

6 Conclusion

IoT information security is a key issue in the development of the IoT. This paper proposed a new mode of IoT information security management based on blockchain. We named it IoTChain, which supports large-scale secure storage of IoT information data, and can authorized legitimate users provide access services. In the IoTChain solution, we used the blockchain to store the encrypted summary information of the original data, and took into account the large-capacity IoT data information, such as images, audio or video captured by the device. We used external flexibility to store raw data information and created a hash id of the content itself and a link to the blockchain. In the IoTChain solution, we proposed efficient and secure authentication, private protection and multi-signature-based conditional traceability methods, so accessed permissions, controlled and constraint information can be easily retrieved from the blockchain. Analysis and performance evaluations show that the IoTChain solution provides reliable, secure, efficient and tamper-proof data information content services. In the future, we will strengthen our work to support the management and trading of IoT data information in the Ethereum-based currency.

References

1. Xu, L.D., Xu, E.L., Li, L.: Industry 4.0: state of the art and future trends. Int. J. Prod. Res. **56**(8), 2941–2962 (2018)
2. Al-Fuqaha, A., et al.: Internet of Things: a survey on enabling technologies, protocols, and applications. IEEE Commun. Surv. Tutor. **17**(4), 2347–2376 (2015)
3. Jing, Q., et al.: Security of the Internet of Things: perspectives and challenges. Wirel. Netw. **20**(8), 2481–2501 (2014)
4. Christidis, K., Devetsikiotis, M.: Blockchains and smart contracts for the Internet of Things. IEEE Access **4**, 2292–2303 (2016)
5. Kshetri, N.: Can blockchain strengthen the Internet of Things? IT Prof. **19**(4), 68–72 (2017)
6. Zheng, Z.B., et al.: Blockchain challenges and opportunities: a survey. Int. J. Web Grid Serv. **14**(4), 352–375 (2018)

7. Gai, K., et al.: Privacy-preserving energy trading using consortium blockchain in smart grid. IEEE Trans. Ind. Inform. **15**(6), 3548–3558 (2019)
8. Zanella, A., et al.: Internet of Things for smart cities. IEEE IInternet Things J. **1**(1), 22–32 (2014)
9. Sharma, P.K., Chen, M.-Y., Park, J.H.: A software defined fog node based distributed blockchain cloud architecture for IoT. IEEE Access **6**, 115–124 (2018)
10. Gai, K., et al.: Security and privacy issues: a survey on fintech, in smart computing and communication. Smartcom **2016**, 236–247 (2017)
11. Zhu, L., et al.: Controllable and trustworthy blockchain-based cloud data management. Futur. Gener. Comput. Syst. Int. J. Escience **91**, 527–535 (2019)
12. Khan, M.A., Salah, K.: IoT security: review, blockchain solutions, and open challenges. Futur. Gener. Comput. Syst. Int. J. Escience **82**, 395–411 (2018)
13. Allam, Z., Dhunny, Z.A.: On big data, artificial intelligence and smart cities. Cities **89**, 80–91 (2019)
14. Tschorsch, F., Scheuermann, B.: Bitcoin and beyond: a technical survey on decentralized digital currencies. IEEE Commun. Surv. Tutor. **18**(3), 2084–2123 (2016)
15. Pustisek, M., Kos, A.: Approaches to front-end IoT application development for the ethereum blockchain. In: Bie, R., Sun, Y., Yu, J. (eds.) 2017 International Conference on Identification, Information and Knowledge in the Internet of Things, pp. 410–419 (2018)
16. Atzori, L., Iera, A., Morabito, G.: The Internet of Things: a survey. Comput. Netw. **54**(15), 2787–2805 (2010)
17. Gubbi, J., et al.: Internet of Things (IoT): a vision, architectural elements, and future directions. Futur. Gener. Comput. Syst. Int. J. Escience **29**(7), 1645–1660 (2013)
18. Botta, A., et al.: Integration of cloud computing and Internet of Things: a survey. Futur. Gener. Comput. Syst. Int. J. Escience **56**, 684–700 (2016)
19. Chen, Y., et al.: An improved P2P file system scheme based on IPFS and blockchain. In: Nie, J.Y., et al. (eds.) 2017 IEEE International Conference on Big Data, pp. 2652–2657 (2017)
20. Wang, S., Zhang, Y., Zhang, Y.: A blockchain-based framework for data sharing with fine-grained access control in decentralized storage systems. IEEE Access **6**, 38437–38450 (2018)
21. Hasan, H.R., Salah, K.: Combating deepfake videos using blockchain and smart contracts. IEEE Access **7**, 41596–41606 (2019)
22. Bogdanov, A., Khovratovich, D., Rechberger, C.: Biclique cryptanalysis of the full AES. In: Lee, D.H., Wang, X. (eds.) ASIACRYPT 2011. LNCS, vol. 7073, pp. 344–371. Springer, Heidelberg (2011). https://doi.org/10.1007/978-3-642-25385-0_19

A Wearable Ad Hoc Device for Situational Awareness and Trusted Collaboration

Zhenyu Guan, Jiawei Li[✉], Hao Liu, and Dawei Li

School of Cyber Science and Technology, Beihang University, Beijing 100191, China
daweix@buaa.edu.cn

Abstract. We develop a new wearable situational awareness and trusted collaboration system to solve several problems with existing wearable devices: a low degree of functional integration and use efficiency, the credibility of data and depending on some external facilities (such as the Internet and servers). We implement a variety of features on a wearable device, improve interaction efficiency by introducing Mixed Reality (MR) to the system. Besides, unlike existing infrastructure-dependent (e.g., for positioning or identification) devices, we use ad hoc network and embedded local modules to reach a offline implementation of information analysis and processing. Moreover, to guarantee the credibility of information in the ad hoc network, we use a lightweight blockchain among the devices. In this way, each device in the network can conduct local situational awareness and instant interaction with the user, and the information passed among users can also be considered credible.

Keywords: Blockchain · Wearable device · Mixed reality · Trusted positioning

1 Introduction

Nowadays, wearable devices mainly concentrate on health care and data reporting [5]. Most of them are designed as an extension of smart phones or other hardware devices, and their tasks (Updating and synchronization data, information transfer, etc.) rely on mobile network or Wi-Fi, which serves as a necessary condition for these wearable devices, becoming a restriction of wider application. Secondly, on situational awareness, existing wearable devices have limited functions, we can do a lot beyond collecting and reporting information about physical activity or sleep patterns, or informing user to pick up the phone. Thirdly, wearable devices don't work as an independent part, it usually collaborates with smart phones or other devices in IoT. So, the credibility of the information transferred among these smart devices needs more consideration. But nowadays, the authentic of the information reported or transferred by wearable devices is not ensured. Moreover, the interaction efficiency of wearable devices still needs to be improved.

© Springer Nature Switzerland AG 2019
M. Qiu (Ed.): SmartBlock 2019, LNCS 11911, pp. 11–20, 2019.
https://doi.org/10.1007/978-3-030-34083-4_2

A wearable device is designed to solve the problems mentioned above. First, It records, analyses and transfers data locally without the support of the Internet or any external servers, getting rid of any external basic facilities. This is supported by two points, one is local embedded modules for specific tasks, and the other is connecting the wearable devices to build an ad hoc network. The collaboration of the nodes in the ad hoc network can extend the information and improve work efficiency of one node. Secondly, not only can our device record the current situation, but give a hand to extract and highlight the key information in the situation. This is implemented by introducing mixed reality (MR) and artificial intelligence (AI). Markers and annotations generated by AI are shown on the purview of the user, which improves the interaction efficiency as well. To assure the data credibility of the system, and in consideration of the devices work in ad hoc network, we employ a lightweight blockchain among the devices. The blockchain works with an identity-based encryption system, serves as a safe pipe for all data transferred and shared among the nodes. Our contributions mainly lie in:

1. In this paper we extend the application of MR to military and police fields by achieving real-time local target detection and trusted positioning on MR devices to support situational awareness and trusted collaboration.
2. Target detection usually requires high-frequency computation and communication. We develop a light-weight embedded module on MR by deploying deep-learning frameworks with pre-training technology. This module is as small as a piece of credit card, and provides efficient and accurate target detection calculated locally, from which the detection results would be shown on MR HMD (Head Mount Display)
3. In this system we utilize the consensus of blockchain to calculate the location information of each nodes and make sure the positioning trusted by more than half nodes of the system.

In this paper, first we introduce related works briefly (Sect. 2). then we describe how the different modules work and link with the others (Sect. 3). Then followed by experiments and tests (Sect. 5). At last, some application scenarios for the system and conclusions are described (Sect. 6).

2   Related Works

At present, there are many security technologies and their corresponding systems exist, such as network video surveillance, access control, alarm information transmission. But all have some limitations such as relying on fixed infrastructure in public facilities, possibilities that data be tampered, the difficulty of free sharing, and limited efficiency of device interaction.

Therefore, we designed a small hub to process data credibly, which works with the HMD and these two combines as a node in an ad hoc network. By extending the field of application of wearable devices, this system provides solutions for the aforementioned security issues.

The technology of blockchain is widely used as the Bitcoin [7] proposed, which has the ability to implement tamper-proofing information records in a network that is going to be centralized. Some research and application about blockchain has been done [1,3,6]. Brambilla et al. [2] based on the consensus mechanism of blockchain, realized the reliability verification of network node position. Based on key updating and blacklist mechanism, we deploy a lightweight blockchain on embedded platform.

3 System Framework

To make it clear, the framework is depicted in Fig. 1.

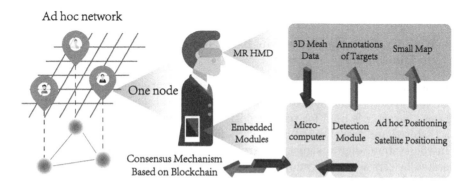

Fig. 1. Framework of the system

It can be divided into four parts in the system: MR HMD, detection module, positioning module, and a microcomputer serves as a data hub and participates in building the blockchain. The HMD is the core of constructing UI to interaction with users. Local-detection makes the system free from relying on the specific conditions of network environment, realizing the goal of real-time detection of presupposed objects defined by specific application scenarios in a low power consumption. When the signal from global satellite is weak or unavailable, the algorithm we proposed can get absolute position approximately from relative positions in relative positioning system. Based on identity, the system contains a high-efficient symmetric encryption model. Trusted ad-hoc network is based on blockchain, which is built by microcomputers in each node. It warrants the credibility of data.

Positioning is implemented by satellite positioning system and relative positioning system. All the positioning or ranging data will be sent to blockchain, then delivered to the HMD.

The HMD uses its camera to grasp real-time frame of the purview, which will be sent to the detecting module by serial communication and receive feedbacks to draw annotations. Data from positioning system will be used for updating the small map in the purview of the user. 3D space mesh data is also shared with other nodes by blockchain.

In this system, a small embedded module will be used as data hub for each node, which serves as a data forwarding node and a node of blockchain. Data transferred between HMD and other modules should be verified, transited and stored on it, if needed.

4   Trusted Positioning

For every node, the positioning modules are connected to a microcomputer, which send data to the HMD, and implement related calculations of packaging and verifying of blocks. Besides the HMD, the microcomputer is another important part of a node.

4.1   Key Updating and Session Key Negotiation Based on Blockchain

Based on embedded platform, we propose an implementation of an ad-hoc system which can update public key and session key in the absence of infrastructure, and this character is used for trusted positioning mainly. Besides, all the other data is stored and transformed by blockchain.

In the system, digital signatures are used to guarantee that information is generated by certain devices and broadcasted. A node first uses identity as public key and uploads it to the blockchain, a private key will be generated by PKG (Private Key Generator). Later, the key updating can be completed by building the key pair of public key and private key independently. The latest public key will always be uploaded to blockchain, which helps to defend replay attacks and for other nodes to require public key in real time. The release and requirement of keys in session key negotiation is based on Diffie-Hellman key exchange protocol. The keys will be update in a certain cycle. By the method proposed above, a high-efficient symmetric encryption model used for our system is built [4].

4.2   Blockchain Implementation on Embedded System

Heretofore, blockchain is rarely built on embedded system. We develop a lightweight model for RPi (Raspberry Pi) independently to implement blockchain.

The Structure of a Block. In the trusted positioning system, a node broadcast its UWB distances, position and updated public key to surrounding nodes. When updating public key, the last public key and the updated key is needed to signature simultaneously to ensure the new public key is generated by trusted node. The structure of a block is shown as Fig. 2.

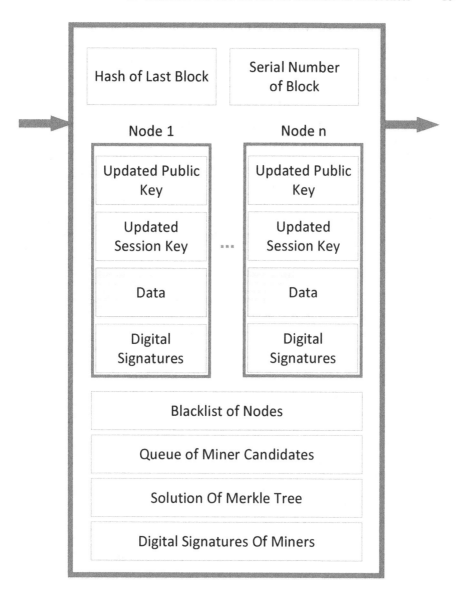

Fig. 2. The Structure of a block

New block is generated by miner, and it has the hash of the last block included. Each block contains node data (position, ranging, 3D-mesh and detection result), updated public key, session key and the digital signature of the node. The blacklist of nodes, the candidate queue of miners is contained as well. A miner hashes all the information in the Merkle tree, and generate the digital signature of the block, and place it in the ending of the block.

Incentive Contract. In the blockchain, the miners generate new blocks. In order to ensure the miners to work in good faith and offset the consumption come from the generating of new blocks, an incentive contract is needed. Unlike the bitcoin system, here we use the punitive mechanism based on blacklist. Suppose that it is of low probability that a pair of adjacent nodes both refuse to generate new block, and there is no multi-hop connection between nodes. To punish the miner who refuse to generate or update new block, we set a blacklist bl in block. In the initial stage of the system, set variables M and B to represent the count of miners and blocks. When a new block is generated, the list ml storage the node count of surrounding nodes of the nodes in the system (descending). The top M nodes (except the current miner) will be the candidates for next cycle. If two nodes generate block at the same time, the system selects the block generated by top-ranked node in the list, and add all the nodes after this node to bl, make it unable to candidate in the generation of new blocks in B block cycles.

The Work Flow of Blockchain

step 1 **Block Verifying.** Assuming that the current mining node is usr_i, the usr_i firstly verifies the signature of the previous block with the public key of usr_{i-1}, and then read Landmark info.

step 2 **Get Position.** In APS system, any nodes can get distances from other nodes by checking signal intensity. By distances between usr_i and other nodes (at least 3), its relative position can be calculated.

step 3 **Block Generating.** usr_i calculates the hash of last block(usr_{i-1}), receives blocks which have been broadcasted but not putted in blockchain, verifies their validity, and proofs the workload.

step 4 **Private key Signature.** Node usr_i signs private key for the hash gotten above, and packages all the info to a temp data pack after finishing the proof the workload.

step 5 **Broadcast Publicly.** The temp data pack is transferred from node usr_i to usr_{i+1}. At the same time, the block contents will be broadcasted to support verifying of other nodes.

step 6 **Node Verifying.** Judge data block branch, receive the verification of other user nodes, verify the existence of spoofing nodes and the legality of blocks.

step 7 **Block Adding.** If node usr_i is a legal node and generates legal block, add this block to the blockchain. Otherwise, if node usr_i is a spoofing one, implement punitive mechanisms and add it to blacklist, and discard the obsolete info.

The workflow is displayed as Fig. 3.

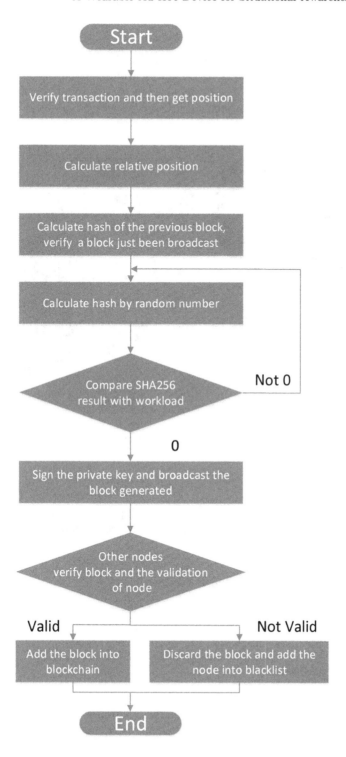

Fig. 3. The work flow of blockchain

5   Experiment

The user interface of the system is designed as Fig. 4 shows. There is a small map in the corner, which shows positions, distances, while adjacent nodes (users) are shown as numbered points. Current 3D space is scanned and transferred when needed, and if there is target detected, annotation will be shown at side.

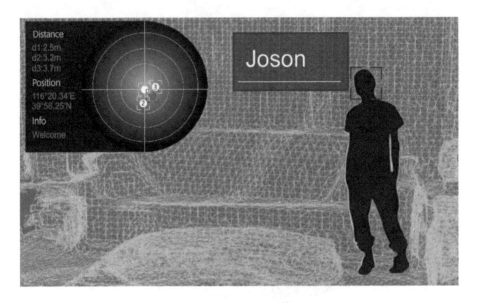

Fig. 4. The user interface

The correct rates of face detection and recognition are shown in Table 1. Each frame has 1 face contained. All faces are in front direction. The weights are trained from face pictures of 83 people for 10 pictures each face. We set the threshold for classification judgments to 85%. The resolution of input images is 896 × 504.

Table 1. Face detection

	Processed frames	Correct frames	Correct rate
Detect	1005	920	91.5%
Recognize	920	864	93.9%[a]

[a]The fail rate results from the probability does not reach the threshold value.

Improvement of lighting conditions in the environment, increase in capture resolution and a better training set can help to enhance the performance of target detection.

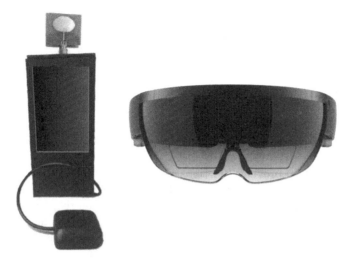

Fig. 5. The appearance of one node

We put all the embedded modules and the microcomputer into a small box. And the appearance of one node is shown in Fig. 5.

Some frames taken from capturing the purview of the HMD are shown in Fig. 6.

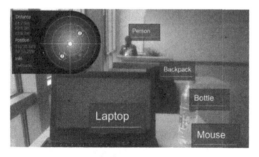

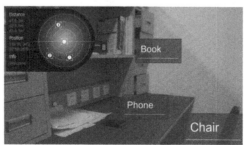

Fig. 6. HMD interface

The small map is generated by relative positioning, working together with the camera projection orientation to rotate. Annotations is refreshed as soon as data received from the detection module.

6   Conclusions

Our system implements all the main characters in Fig. 1. By combining multiple modules and technologies, the platform gains a wide range of application prospects.

As a system which provides functions of real-time or asynchronous space collaboration, important target detection, information exchange and trusted positioning, it can be used in scenarios where security is required. Besides, thanks to the application of MR, users can grasp all the information in a convenient way, so efficiency is another advantage of the system. The application scenarios include but are not limited to fighting against earthquake and relieving disaster, firefighting, anti-terrorism and enforcement.

References

1. Ahmed, K., Andrew, M., Elaine, S., Zikai, W., Charalampos, P.: Hawk: the blockchain model of cryptography and privacy-preserving smart contracts. In: Security & Privacy, pp. 839–858 (2016)
2. Giacomo, B., Michele, A., Francesco, Z.: Using block chain for peer-to-peer proof-of-location (2016)
3. Guy, Z., Oz, N., 'Sandy', P.A.: Decentralizing privacy: using blockchain to protect personal data. In: IEEE Security & Privacy Workshops, pp. 180–184 (2015)
4. Li, D.-W., Liu, J.-W., Guan, Z.-Y., Qin, Y.-Y., Wu, Q.-H.: Key update and trusted positioning system based on blockchain. J. Cryptologic Res. **5**(1), 35–42 (2018)
5. Ranck, J.: The wearable computing market: a global analysis. Gigaom Pro (2012)
6. Juan, G., Aggelos, K., Nikos, L.: The bitcoin backbone protocol: analysis and applications, pp. 281–310 (2015)
7. Nakamoto, S.: Bitcoin: a peer-to-peer electronic cash system (2008). https://bitcoin.org/bitcoin.pdf

Distributed Audit System of SDN Controller Based on Blockchain

Zhenyu Guan[1], Hanzheng Lyu[1], Haibin Zheng[2], Dawei Li[1(✉)],
and Jianwei Liu[1]

[1] School of Cyber Science and Technology, Beihang University, Beijing 100191, China
lidawei@buaa.edu.cn
[2] School of Electronic and Information Engineering,
Beihang University, Beijing 100191, China

Abstract. In the existing Software-Defined Networking (SDN), the network infrastructure is divided into different network domains according to the operators assigned to it. In this paper, by adding monitor meta to the switch layer, the flow table rules and logs issued by the controller are distributed recorded. The consortium blockchain is constructed by distributed secret sharing scheme, and the consensus mechanism based on blockchain ensures the validity and traceability of flow table rules of the controller, providing non-tampering service and cost records for multiparty operators without using a trusted third party. The system is designed to solve the problem of auditing and accounting in the untrusted environment in SDN and it has good security and reliability that is suitable for deployment in the actual SDN network.

Keywords: SDN · Auditing of controller · Blockchain · Secret sharing · Distributed key generation

1 Introduction

Network communication has become one of the important infrastructures for modern social development and technological progress. The urgent demand of mass data processing and new types of Internet services have made the traditional network structure increasingly incapable of meeting the needs of today's enterprises, operators and users. Software-Defined Networking [7] have attracted widespread attention as a new network architecture.

The controller is the core device in the SDN network architecture, which is responsible for centralized management and control of the status and topology

This work is supported by the National Key Research and Development Program of China through project 2016YFC1000307, by the National Natural Science Foundation of China through projects 61702028, 61672083, 61370190,61772538, 61532021, 61472429, and 61402029, by the foundation of Science and Technology on Information Assurance Laboratory through project 1421120305162112006, by the National Cryptography Development Fund through project MMJJ20170106.

M. Qiu (Ed.): SmartBlock 2019, LNCS 11911, pp. 21–31, 2019.
https://doi.org/10.1007/978-3-030-34083-4_3

information of the entire network [3,4]. Onix [6] is a distributed controller that was proposed early, a large number of distributed controllers followed, such as Hyperflow [15], ONOS [1], and Kandoo [5]. At the same time, Phemius et al. [10] proposed a multi domain distributed SDN network architecture in 2014, which divides the entire network into multiple distributed domains.

When communication is performed between users belonging to different network domains, or when a data path of a network application spans multiple network domains, data protection become critical [11,12], and the architecture of the cross domain communication system is shown in Fig. 1. It can be seen from the figure that there are the following problems in the process of cross-domain communication: (1) It is difficult to guarantee the quality of service and the degree of completion of inter-operator data communication services; (2) It is difficult for operators to perform cost audits.

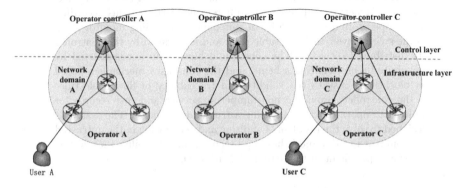

Fig. 1. Cross-domain communication system architecture

In this paper, the controller is added to the switch layer. Using consensus algorithm and distributed key generation technology, a distributed audit system in the form of consortium blockchain suitable for distributed SDN network is designed. Blockchain-based SDN distributed auditing system has non-defective modification and unforgeability. The system generates publicly untraceable log record chains to implement the audit function for the controller to issue flow table behavior.

In the following part of this paper, Sect. 2 gives a brief overview of the knowledge used in building SDN Distributed Auditing System; Sect. 3 outlines the model structure and the implementation of the system; Sect. 4 analyzes the correctness, security, and efficiency of the designed system; Sect. 5 summarizes this paper.

2   Related Work

2.1   SDN System Architecture

The typical architecture of the SDN system is divided into three layers: application layer, control layer, and infrastructure layer. The top layer is the application layer, including different types of services and applications. The middle layer is the control layer and is mainly responsible for the centralized management and control of the status and topology information of the entire network. On the one hand, it communicates with the infrastructure layer through the southbound interface to implement resource layout of the data plane; on the other hand, it provides an extensible programming interface to the application layer through the northbound interface. At the bottom is the infrastructure layer, which is composed of forwarding devices at the bottom of the network and is mainly responsible for data processing, forwarding, and status collection.

2.2   Blockchain

Blockchain is a decentralized infrastructure gradually rising with the increasing popularity of digital cryptocurrencies such as Bitcoin [8]. After several years of development and improvement, blockchain has gradually become a new type of distributed, decentralized, and detrusted technology solution [13, 16].

The blockchain is composed of data blocks and chained structures. A block consists of a series of data blocks generated by cryptography. The block head of each block contains the hash value of the previous block. Blocks are linked by such hash values to previous block to form a chain. At the same time, the data block is time stamped to form a chain structure to record the complete history of blockchain data. Blockchain has five main characteristics: decentralization, openness, independence, tamper-resistant and permanent.

2.3   Distributed Key Generation

Secret sharing is an important part of the threshold cryptosystem. Its concept was first proposed by Shamir [14] and Blakley [2] in 1979 based on the Lagrangian difference and the projective geometric theorem respectively. The use of secret sharing schemes to keep secret information helps prevent the excessive concentration of power on the one hand and the security and integrity of the secret information on the other. At present, the most widely used distributed key generation protocol based on discrete logarithms is the DKG protocol based on Feldman-VSS [17] and Pedersen-VSS [9] secret sharing.

3   SDN Distributed Audit System Model

In order to implement the supervision of the behavior of the controller in the SDN network, this paper proposes a blockchain-based SDN controller distributed

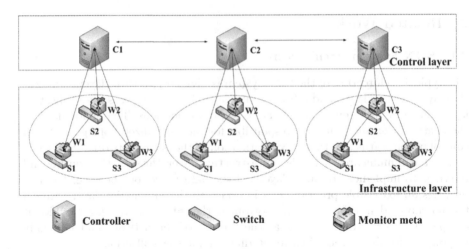

Fig. 2. The system architecture

auditing system. The system architecture is shown in Fig. 2. The deployment of distributed monitoring devices is performed at the switch level of the SDN architecture to realize the audit function of the controller.

The blockchain-based SDN controller distributed audit system constructed by the project mainly includes four parts: system initialization, distributed records, consensus reach and consortium blockchain generation.

S1. System Initialization: The switch device is defined as $S_1, S_2, \cdots, S_n$. The flow table and log information it receives are from controller $C_1, C_2, \cdots, C_m$. The deployment monitor meta $W_1, W_2, \cdots, W_n$ enters the switch cluster. The system output the generated public parameter *param*. The Watchers take turns to be the dominant miner and is responsible for collecting all valid log records broadcasted during the period.

Let the system be a discrete logarithm based public key system with a parameter of (p, q, g, h). p,q is a large prime number, $q|(p-1)$, $\mathbb{G}_q$ is the only q-order subgroup of $\mathbb{Z}_p^*$, g,h are generators of $\mathbb{G}_q$, and it is impossible to compute the discrete logarithm $log_g h$. Participants are a group formed by n monitor meta $W_1, W_2, \cdots, W_n$. There is a monotonic access structure Γ on $W = \{W_1, W_2, \cdots, W_n\}$, and $\Gamma = \{T_1, T_2, \cdots, T_t\}$ is the base of Γ. The public parameters (p, q, g, h) are generated by the governing meta-group in some open manner or by a trusted third party.

S2. Distributed Records: Each Watcher $W_1, W_2, \cdots, W_n$ collects the flow table rules and log records delivered by the controller to the corresponding switch in this period (for example, within 10 min) to the local flow table record list, and uses the ECDSA signature algorithm to digitally sign its own record, then broadcasts it to the remaining Watchers. Other Watchers perform signature verification on the ECDSA signatures of each Watcher $W_1, W_2, \cdots, W_n$ to verify the validity of the log sheet.

Let ECDSA signature algorithm system parameters are F_q, E, G, a, b, N, H, where F_q is a finite field, E is an elliptic curve on F_q, G is a base point on E, The order of G is N (N is a prime number), a, b are coefficient of elliptic curve E, H is a one-way safe hash function. Let the key pair of the monitor meta W_i be $(wpk_i, wsk_i) = (Q, d)$, where the log message to be signed is m. The specific signature process is as follows:

(1) Select a random number k, $1 \leq k \leq N - 1$;
(2) Calculate $k \cdot G = (x_1, y_1)$;
(3) Calculate $r = x_1 \bmod N$, if $r = 0$, return to step(1);
(4) Calculate $e = H(m)$, $s = k^{-1}(e + dr)$, if $s = 0$, return to step(1);
(5) The generated monitor meta has the signature $\sigma = (r, s)$ for the log message m.

Finally, the flow table record generated after the monitor meta W_i signed is shown in Fig. 3.

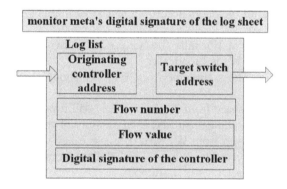

Fig. 3. The flow table record sheet of mintor meta

The monitor meta W_i then broadcasts the signature to the remaining monitor meta. Other monitor meta perform signature verification on the ECDSA signature of each monitor meta $W_1, W_2, \cdots, W_n$. Among them, the signature verification operation of the monitor meta W_j is as follows:

(1) After obtaining the signature $\sigma = (r, s)$, calculate $e = H(m)$, $w = s^{-1} \bmod N$;
(2) Calculate $u_1 = ew \bmod N$, $u_2 = rw \bmod N$, $u_1 G + u_2 Q = (x_0, y_0)$;
(3) Calculate $v = x_0 \bmod N$;
(4) If $v = r$, the signature passes the verification, otherwise the verification fails.

S3. Consensus Reached: Input the system public parameter *param*, and the duty Watcher (miner) generates a quasi-block and publishes it. Consensus agreement between Watchers relies on distributed secret sharing and key generation protocols. Each Watcher $W_1, W_2, \cdots, W_n$ runs a distributed key generation protocol and calculates the shared key sk and the public key pk required to generate the consortium blockchain.

1. Quasi-block generation

   The miner collects all log records broadcast during the time period, performs ECDSA signature and SHA-256 hash operation (the specific process is the same as step S2), and generates a quasi-block.

2. Generation of shared keys and their own private keys

   Input system common parameters (p, q, g, h), each monitor meta $W_1, W_2, \cdots,$ W_n runs a VSS-based distributed key generation protocol to form a consortium blockchain. $x \in Z_q$ indicates the private key to be generated by the consortium blockchain formed by monitor metas, and $y = g^x (\mathrm{mod}\, p)$ indicates the corresponding public key in consortium blockchain. The distributed key generation protocol in the scheme refers to the distributed key generation based on generalized verifiable secret sharing by Zhang et al. [17].

   (1) Each member W_j of the group W randomly chooses one element x_j according to the uniform distribution, and shares x_j as the access structure Γ among all members according to the verifiable secret sharing protocol.

   (2) If the validation of W_k fails (i.e. (x_{jk}, e_{jk}) is invalid), (x_{jk}, e_{jk}) and a complaint about W_j is broadcast.

   (3) After receiving the complaint from W_k, W_j should broadcast its valid share to W_k.

   (4) If the broadcast share from W_j in step 3 is still invalid or complained by all members of a qualified subset, each member of the subset replaces the share it has received from W_j with 0, $x_{jk} = e_{jk} = 0$, which is equivalent to treating x_j selected by W_j as 0, and the polynomials $F_j(x)$ and $G_j(x)$ as zero polynomials.

   (5) Members of a subset calculate their share about x: $s_k = x_{1k} + x_{2k} + \cdots + x_{nk} (\mathrm{mod}\, q)$, $u_k = e_{1k} + e_{2k} + \cdots + e_{nk} (\mathrm{mod}\, q)$. The generated shared private key is $x = x_1 + x_2 + \cdots + x_n (\mathrm{mod}\, q)$.

   $sk = x$.

3. Extraction of the public key in consortium blockchain

   According to the generated shared private key, the commonly generated public key $y = g^x (\mathrm{mod}\, p)$ can be extracted. The specific process is as follows:

   (1) Each member of the subset W_k broadcasts $A_{ki} = g^{F_{ki}} (\mathrm{mod}\, p)$, $i = 0, 1, 2, \cdots, n - 1$.

   (2) Each member W_j verifies the validity of broadcast data $A_{ki} = g^{F_{ki}}$ from W_k, i.e. check whether there is $g^{x_{kj}} = \prod_{i=0}^{n-1} A_{ki}^{j^i}$, $j = 1, 2, \cdots, n$.

   (3) Each member of the subset W_j calculates its own public key $y_j = A_{j0} = g^{F_{j0}} (\mathrm{mod}\, p)$, $j = 1, 2, \cdots, n$.

   (4) Finally, the public key corresponding to the shared private key is generated as $y = \prod_{j=1}^{n} y_j (\mathrm{mod}\, p)$.

   $pk = y$.

S4. Consortium Blockchain Generation: The miner digitally signs the flow table records that have been verified through the verification using the secret value sk shared by the parties, and packages and generates the latest block. Other monitor metas use the consortium blockchain public key pk for signature verification. The specific process is shown in Fig. 4.

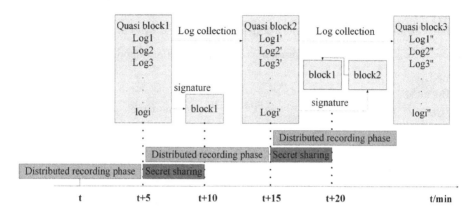

Fig. 4. Consortium blockchain generation process

1. Block generation
   The duty monitor meta uses the shared key sk and ECDSA signature algorithm to make the quasi-block a new block by signature (the specific process is the same as step S2).
2. Block join
   All other monitor metas use the consortium blockchain public key pk for signature verification (the specific process is the same as step S2). If the verification passes, the block is added to the existing blockchain, and the latest blockchain is updated and generated.

   When abnormal data occurs or the cross-domain flow table is issued for payment, the generated blockchain information may be invoked to audit the flow table rules and log records.

4   System Analysis

4.1   Correctness

The construction of the scheme in this paper is based on cryptographic protocols such as ECDSA digital signature and distributed key generation and blockchain mechanism.

For the ECDSA digital signature algorithm in the system, if the equation $v = r$ is satisfied, the signature is verified.

Because $v = x_0 \bmod n$, $r = x_1 \bmod n$,

$u_1 G + u_2 Q = (x_0, y_0)$, $k \cdot G = (x_1, y_1)$, at this time,

$$u_1 G + u_2 Q = ewG + rwQ = (ew + rwd)G = (e + rd)s^{-1}G = kG$$

So $v = r$ is satisfied.

Conclusion 1: The effective signature on the logbook of the monitor meta in the system depends on the correctness of the ECDSA digital signature.

For the distributed key generation protocol in the system, if the equation $E_{jk} = E(x_{jk}, e_{jk}) = \prod_{i=0}^{n-1} E_{ji}^{k^i}$ and $g^{x_{kj}} = \prod_{i=0}^{n-1} A_{ki}^{j^i}$ is satisfied, the protocol is verified.

Because

$E_{jk} = E(x_{jk}, e_{jk}) = g^{x_{jk}} h^{e_{jk}} = g^{F_j(k)} h^{G_j(k)}$, at this time,

$$\prod_{i=0}^{n-1} E_{ji}^{k^i} = g^{F_{j0}} h^{G_{j0}} \cdot g^{kF_{j1}} h^{kG_{j1}} \cdots g^{k^{n-1}F_{jn-1}} h^{k^{n-1}G_{jn-1}} = g^{F_j(k)} h^{G_j(k)}$$

So $E_{jk} = \prod_{i=0}^{n-1} E_{ji}^{k^i}$ is satisfied.

Similarly, there are

$$\prod_{i=0}^{n-1} A_{ki}^{j^i} = g^{F_{k0}} \cdot g^{jF_{k1}} \cdot g^{j^2 F_{k2}} \cdots g^{j^{n-1}F_{kn-1}} = g^{F_k(j)} = g^{x_{kj}}$$

So $g^{x_{kj}} = \prod_{i=0}^{n-1} A_{ki}^{j^i}$ is satisfied.

Conclusion 2: The correctly achieve of consensus of each monitor meta and the generation of the consortium blockchain in the system depend on the validity of the distributed key generation protocol.

4.2   Security

The security of the system mainly depends on the security algorithm and consensus algorithm adopted by the system. The digital signature algorithm uses the existing standard signature algorithm ECDSA and the hash function algorithm uses the existing security standard SHA-256. The consensus reach algorithm adopts the distributed key generation protocol based on generalized VSS in [17]. The miner-generated quasi-blocks can only generate the corresponding public-private key pairs and be digitally signed if they are approved by more than half of the nodes and share secret shares. After being approved by the majority of the nodes of the consortium blockchain network, it is finally added to the blockchain. Any tampered or forged information will be difficult to reach consensus by more than half of the nodes, thus ensuring the security of the system information.

Conclusion 3: Assuming that the ECDSA signature algorithm and the distributed key generation protocol used in the system are secure, the system can operate securely when the number of attackers in the system is less than 51%.

4.3 Efficiency Analysis

The efficiency of this system mainly depends on the efficiency of the algorithm in the process of distributed records, consensus reach, and consortium blockchain generation. We let τ_m be the time required to perform a multiplication operation on the elliptic curve E in the ECDSA digital signature algorithm, τ_d represents the time required to perform a multiplication operation, t_m represents the time required to perform a multiplication operation on the group $\mathbb{G}$, t_e represents the time required to perform an exponential operation, and t_h represents the time required to perform a hash function SHA256. The number of monitor meta in the consortium blockchain is n, and the number of flow table records generated in each time period is m. Table 1 shows the time required in each stage of the system.

Table 1. System calculation efficiency analysis

System phase	Functional requirements	Time required
Distributed records T_D	ECDSA signature $T_S = \lceil \log_2 k \rceil \tau_d + 2\tau_m + t_h$ $T_V = (\lceil \log_2 u_1 \rceil + \lceil \log_2 u_2 \rceil)\tau_d + 3\tau_m + t_h$	$T_D = m \cdot (T_S + T_V)$
Consensus reached T_C	Quasi-block generation $T_Z = T_S + 2t_h$ Generation of shared keys and their own private keys $T_K =$ $T_V + (5n-1)t_e + (2n^2 + 8n + 3)t_m$ Consortium blockchain public key extraction $T_P = (4n-2)t_e + (2n-1)t_m$	$T_G = T_Z + T_K + T_P$
Consortium blockchain generation T_G	Block generation $T_B = T_S$ Block join $T_P = T_V$	$T_U = T_B + T_P$

According to the analysis of the calculation efficiency of each stage of the system in Table 1, we can get the total time-consuming of the block generation process in this system:

$$T = T_D + T_G + T_U$$
$$= (m+2)((\lceil \log_2 k \rceil + \lceil \log_2 u_1 \rceil + \lceil \log_2 u_2 \rceil)\tau_d + 5\tau_m + 2t_h) + (9n-3)t_e$$
$$+ (2n^2 + 10n + 2)t_m + 2t_h$$

Therefore, this system has high computational efficiency and low requirements for computational performance. It is suitable for deployment in practical applications.

5   Conclusion

Implementing effective audit supervision of the controller in the SDN network has important practical significance. Based on the blockchain mechanism, this paper designs a blockchain-based SDN controller distributed auditing system by adding monitor meta at the switch layer, adopting ECDSA signature algorithm and distributed key generation protocol. In this paper, the system is designed rationally, and the functions of distributed recording, consensus building and consortium blockchain generation are realized. At the same time, the concrete realization of these three modules is integrated and applied. With the continuous development of SDN network technology, the controller distributed audit system will play an active role in the multi-operator auditing and cross-domain billing.

References

1. Berde, P., et al.: ONOS: towards an open, distributed SDN OS. In: Proceedings of the Third Workshop on Hot Topics in Software Defined Networking, pp. 1–6. ACM (2014)
2. Blakley, G.R., et al.: Safeguarding cryptographic keys. In: Proceedings of the National Computer Conference, vol. 48, pp. 313–317 (1979)
3. Chen, L., Qiu, M., Dai, W., Jiang, N.: Supporting high-quality video streaming with SDN-based CDNs. J. Supercomput. **73**(8), 3547–3561 (2017)
4. Chen, L., Qiu, M., Xiong, J.: An SDN-based fabric for flexible data-center networks. In: 2015 IEEE 2nd International Conference on Cyber Security and Cloud Computing, pp. 121–126. IEEE (2015)
5. Hassas Yeganeh, S., Ganjali, Y.: Kandoo: a framework for efficient and scalable offloading of control applications. In: Proceedings of the First Workshop on Hot Topics in Software Defined Networks, pp. 19–24. ACM (2012)
6. Koponen, T., et al.: Onix: a distributed control platform for large-scale production networks. In: OSDI, vol. 10, pp. 1–6 (2010)
7. McKeown, N.: Software-defined networking. INFOCOM Keynote Talk **17**(2), 30–32 (2009)
8. Nakamoto, S., et al.: Bitcoin: a peer-to-peer electronic cash system (2008)
9. Pedersen, T.P.: A threshold cryptosystem without a trusted party. In: Davies, D.W. (ed.) EUROCRYPT 1991. LNCS, vol. 547, pp. 522–526. Springer, Heidelberg (1991). https://doi.org/10.1007/3-540-46416-6_47
10. Phemius, K., Bouet, M., Leguay, J.: Disco: Distributed multi-domain SDN controllers. In: 2014 IEEE Network Operations and Management Symposium (NOMS), pp. 1–4. IEEE (2014)
11. Qiu, H., Kapusta, K., Lu, Z., Qiu, M., Memmi, G.: All-or-nothing data protection for ubiquitous communication: Challenges and perspectives. Inf. Sci. **502**, 434–445 (2019)
12. Qiu, H., Noura, H., Qiu, M., Ming, Z., Memmi, G.: A user-centric data protection method for cloud storage based on invertible dwt. IEEE Trans. Cloud Comput. (2019)
13. Qiu, H., Qiu, M., Memmi, G., Ming, Z., Liu, M.: A dynamic scalable blockchain based communication architecture for IoT. In: Qiu, M. (ed.) SmartBlock 2018. LNCS, vol. 11373, pp. 159–166. Springer, Cham (2018). https://doi.org/10.1007/978-3-030-05764-0_17

14. Shamir, A.: How to share a secret. Commun. ACM **22**(11), 612–613 (1979)
15. Tootoonchian, A., Ganjali, Y.: HyperFlow: a distributed control plane for Open-Flow. In: Proceedings of the 2010 Internet Network Management Conference on Research on Enterprise Networking, p. 3 (2010)
16. Y, Y.: The work of Bitcoin mechanism (2013)
17. Zhang, F.t., Wang, Y.m.: Distributed key generation based on generalized verifiable secret sharing. Acta electronica Sinica **31**(4), 580–584 (2003)

Food Supply Chain Traceability Scheme Based on Blockchain and EPC Technology

Haihui Huang[1], Xiuxiu Zhou[1(✉)], and Jun Liu[2]

[1] School of Communication and Information Engineering,
Chongqing University of Posts and Telecommunications, Chongqing, China
huanghh@cqupt.edu.cn, s170131122@stu.cqupt.edu.cn
[2] School of Software Engineering, Chongqing University of Posts
and Telecommunications, Chongqing, China

Abstract. In order to effectively detect and prevent food safety issues and track responsibilities, it is indispensable to establish a reliable traceable system. Accurate recording, sharing and tracking of specific data in food production, processing, warehousing, transportation and retailing is particularly important throughout the food supply chain. This paper proposes a safe food traceable scheme based on blockchain and EPC technology. Encoding food by EPC technology, using the Ethernet block chain and smart contract to effectively execute transactions, manage all transactions among participants involved in the supply chain ecosystem, to track and trace food in the entire agricultural supply chain. In addition, a data management system structure combining on-chain and off-chain is proposed, which uses IPFS to store data under the chain, to alleviate the data explosion in the block chain of the Internet of Things. Which provide safe, efficient and transparent food traceable scheme.

Keywords: Food traceability · Blockchain · Smart contract · EPC · IPFS

1 Introduction

Product traceability is an indispensable means of modern supply management and a key technology to solve food safety problem [1]. At present, the mainstream product traceability system is mainly controlled by government departments or a core enterprise [2], traceability records are processed by a department or company. This traditional

This work is supported by the National Natural Science Foundation (Grant No. 61772099, 61772098); the Program for Innovation Team Building at Institutions of Higher Education in Chongqing (Grant No. CXTDG201602010); Chongqing Science and Technology Innovation Leadership Support Program (Grant No. CSTCCXLJRC201917); the University Outstanding Achievements Transformation Funding Project of Chongqing (Grant No. KJZH17116); the Artificial Intelligence Technology Innovation Important Subject Projects of Chongqing (cstc2017rgzn-zdyf0140); The Innovation and Entrepreneurship Demonstration Team Cultivation Plan of Chongqing (cstc2017kjrc-cxcytd0063); the Chongqing Research Program of Basic Research and Frontier Technology (Grant No. cstc2017jcyjAX0270, Grant No. cstc2018jcyjA0672, Grant No. cstc2017jcyjAX0071); the Industry Important Subject Projects of Chongqing (Grant No. CSTC2018JSZX-CYZTZX0178, Grant No. CSTC2018JSZX-CYZTZX0185).

© Springer Nature Switzerland AG 2019
M. Qiu (Ed.): SmartBlock 2019, LNCS 11911, pp. 32–42, 2019.
https://doi.org/10.1007/978-3-030-34083-4_4

traceability system has the following hidden dangers: information tampering, label copy, accountability difficult, spamming Products.

To solve the above hidden dangers, many companies, governments [3, 4] and related researchers and technology companies have proposed solutions based on blockchain technology. Xu et al. [5] designed a blockchain-based traceable system originChain, which reconstructs the current system by replacing the central database with blockchain, and provides high-availability transparent tamper-proof traceability data for originChain. Abeyratne [6] prospected the application of block chain technology in supply chain management, and analyses the possible problems in supply chain management. Niya et al. [7] employed SC on the Ethereum blockchain (BC), their Decentralized Application provided a hardware-and platform-independent approach that flexibly enables multiple object combinations and transformations to be tracked with a use case-agnostic design and utilization. Kentaroh et al. [8] used the Ethereum architecture to create a blockchain smart contract model for supply chain management, and designed a project-level smart contract to manage event information for products in the supply chain. Tian [9] constructed a traceability system based on RFID technology and blockchain to prevent the tracing system information from being tampered with. To protect data privacy, Zyskind et al. [10] have established a blockchain-based personal data management system to ensure users protect data privacy in a distributed situation. Zhu et al. [11] proposed a controllable blockchain data management (CBDM) model that can be deployed in a cloud environment. Gai et al. [12] presented a consortium blockchain-oriented approach to solve the problem of privacy leakage without restricting trading functions. Gai, Wu et al. [13] proposed a model Permissioned Blockchain Edge Model for Smart Grid Network (PBEM-SGN) to address the two significant issues in smart grid, privacy protections and energy security, by means of combining blockchain and edge computing techniques.

From the above research, the main problems of block chain traceability schemes at present are small scale, small number of nodes on the chain, low traceability efficiency, imperfect design of intelligent contracts, and data explosion caused by data overload. To solve the above problems, this paper proposes a collaborative food safety traceability scheme based on block chain and EPC coding.

The main contributions of this paper are as follows: (1) We proposed a safe food traceability solution based on block chain and EPC technology to prevent data tampering, improve traceability accuracy. (2) Applying IPFS to store data under the chain, we can alleviate the data explosion on the block chain by dynamically managing the data on and off the chain. (3) Manage transactions on the chain by deploying smart contracts, through authentication to prevent disclosure of sensitive information, improve the efficiency of traceability and security.

The rest of this article is organized as follows. Sect. 2 introduces the related techniques of the blockchain traceability scheme; Sect. 3 describes the system architecture and data flow on the chain; Sect. 4 describes the algorithmic design of smart contracts in the supply chain, Sect. 5 analyses the performance of smart contracts. Finally, Sect. 6 analyses the experimental results.

2 Related Technology

2.1 EPC Technology

The EPC [14] system is based on computer Internet and radio frequency technology RFID. It applies EPC coding technology to uniquely encode each entity object, and construct an "Internet of Things" that realizes real-time sharing of global item information. The core idea of the EPC system is to scan the electronic tag by radio frequency identification technology, read the unique identifier EPC code of the entity object in the tag, complete the data collection, and obtain the EPC code by the RFID and then transmit the code to the server connected to the Internet to Store and query subsequent data.

2.2 IPFS

IPFS is a point-to-point distributed hypermedia distribution protocol. IPFS is based on content addressing, saving information to IPFS nodes, and the IPFS system will return a unique hash value calculated based on this information. The hash value corresponds to the content of the message, and even if the information is slightly modified, a completely different hash value will be obtained. When IPFS is requested for a file hash, it uses a distributed hash table to find the node where the file is located, gets the file and verifies the file data [15].

2.3 Ethereum

Ethereum [16] is a blockchain development platform that supports smart contracts and lowers the threshold for users to build blockchain applications. Just like Bitcoin, Ethereum is an open source blockchain [17] underlying system. In addition, one of the biggest features of Ethereum is the combination of smart contracts, trustless, no tampering. It provides a credible execution environment for the operation of smart contracts.

3 Design of Traceability Scheme

3.1 Traceability Architecture Design

The traceability scheme is mainly composed of producer users, distributors, regulators and consumers. Manufacturer users combine EPC technology to capture and manage key traceability information for their products. The entire system architecture is shown in Fig. 1. The manufacturer node server consists of five modules whose functions are described in detail as follows:

- EPC Traceability Information Collection Module: This module is designed to collect key traceability information generated during food production, storage, and distribution. Relevant data can be automatically collected by RFID or staffed to identify.

- Event Information Database: This database is mainly used to save and manage all food information in the information collection module.
- Effective Information Extraction Module: This module is mainly used to extract information that needs to be uploaded the blockchain from the traceability information database, and prepare to upload data.
- Blockchain Module: The blockchain module has two functions. One is data interaction, including key traceability information for uploading blockchains, requests for information on the chain, and verification of event information. The other is to provide the user with the option to become a complete blockchain node or a lightweight blockchain node, which is to decide whether to participate in the maintenance of the blockchain.
- Interaction Rights Management Module: When there is any event information interaction, the module is responsible for the verification of the user identity, that is, whether the requestor that initiated the event information request is in the supply chain.

Traceability client consists of two modules:

- Blockchain Module: This module is designed for the link between the client and the system. It can request the information of the blockchain and verify the legitimacy of the information. Select a light node for the module to reduce user maintenance costs.
- Information Cache Database: This cache database is used to cache the corresponding food traceability data tracked by the user.

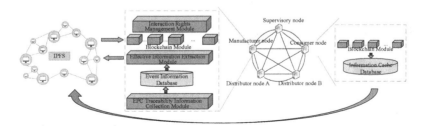

Fig. 1. Food traceability scheme architecture based on blockchain and EPCIS

3.2 Data Flow on the Chain

The system's data flow includes the process of uploading data to the blockchain, the interaction of offline data and consumer queries. The design of these two processes is as follows:

1. Process of Data Uploading to Blockchain
   (1) Food producer A produces food and assigns a unique identifier, The collection of event data for the food is done by the data collection module of A's enterprise user server, and then A will store the collected information by traceability information database.

(2) A extracts key traceability information through the information extraction module, and stores in local database.

(3) A will put relevant certification documents and the manufacturer's detailed information in the local database, encrypt the information and upload it to IPFS.

(4) A call the smart contract writes the encrypted file and traceability information into the block, and automatically generate A's smart contract transaction through the blockchain module. When the peer-to-peer (P2P) network accepts the transaction and successfully uploads it to the blockchain, the manufacturer will transfer the goods.

(5) When dealer B receives these products, it is necessary to verify the legality of the goods by initiating a discovery service request to the corresponding manufacturer A's smart contract. If B is verified, the blockchain module will return the encrypted information hash of A and the server IP address or URL of A.

(6) Distributor B uses the hash value returned by IPFS to query, obtains the encrypted detailed information, and submits its identifier to the manufacturer's server to initiate a request for event data to share the product from A. It compares the hash value with the encrypted hash of A in local database, so we can know whether the data has been tampered with and obtain the detection information of the food.

2. Consumer Inquiry

The detailed process of event data interaction for consumer queries can be divided into six steps:

(1) After receiving the product, the retailer submits the product identification code and the address of the smart contract to the blockchain to request the information discovery service.

(2) The smart contract judges the identity of the requester. Once confirmed, the smart contract will return the manufacturer's server address and encrypted information to the retailer.

(3) The retailer initiates a request for event data to the manufacturer's server and submits its identity (including the public key and the digital signature created by its private key).

(4) The interactive rights management module of the manufacturer server initiates a rights verification request to the smart contract.

(5) The smart contract judges the retailer's authority and returns the result.

(6) According to the judgment of the smart contract, the interactive rights management module determines whether to return the event data (Fig. 2).

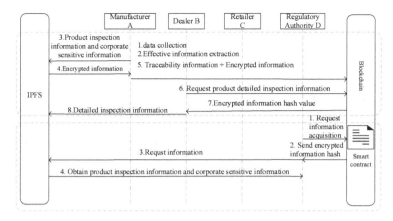

Fig. 2. Data writing and query process

4   Trading Contract Design

4.1   Entity Relationship

To ensure that products are safely tracked using Ethereum Smart Contracts and all participants participate in the process, the manufacturer produces the product and maintains the detailed process in the product production process. Manufacturers record the details of product production in a decentralized file system through IPFS and store the IPFS hash of related files in smart contracts.

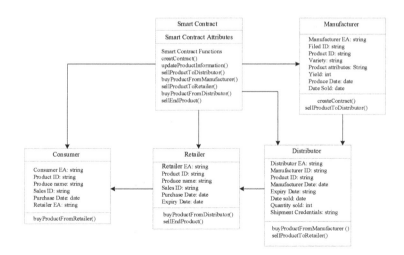

Fig. 3. Entity relationship diagram

The distributor purchases the finished product from manufacturer to ship the product to buyers. After that, the dealer sells the product to the retailer. Figure 3 shows the entity relationship diagram, illustrating the smart contract attributes and functions and the relationship between participating entities and smart contracts.

4.2   Transaction Algorithm Design

In this section, we describe an algorithm that defines how our proposed blockchain-based approach works. As mentioned earlier, manufacturers have created smart contracts. Then it agrees to the purchase terms with a registered distribution company. Algorithm 1 describes the process by which a manufacturer sells a product to a distributor. After the initial state of the contract is established, the smart contract checks to confirm that the requesting distribution company has registered and paid the price of the product. If the plan is successful, the contract status will change to *SeedRequestSubmitted*, the distributor status will change to *WaitForProduct*, and the manufacturer status will change to *AgreeToSell*. The contract notifies the change in the entity activity in the owner chain, otherwise the contract status and other activity participants will return to the initial state and the transaction will terminate.

Algorithm 1 Manufacturer sells product to Distributor

Input: *D is the list of registered Distributor*

   Etherenumaddress(EA) of Distributor,

   Etherenumaddress(EA) of Manufacturer,

   DateManufactured, Quantity , ProductPrice

1 Contractstate is **Created**

2 State of the Distributor *is **ProductsRequested***

3 Manufacturer state is **Ready**

4 Restrict access to only $f \in F$ i.e., registered Distributors

5 if Distributor = *registered and ProductPrice = paid* **then**

6   Contract state changes to *ProductRequestSubmitted*

7   Change State of the *Distributor* to *WaitForProduct*

8   Manufacturer state is *AgreeToSell*

9   Create a notification message stating sale of product

10 end

11 else

12   Revert contract state and show an error.

13 end

Once the distributor receives the product, it can sell it to the retailer. As shown in Algorithm 2, At this stage, the contract status is *ProductSoldToDistributor* and the distributor status is *ProductReceived-FromManufacturer*. The retailer's status is *ReadyToPurchase*.

Contract restrictions can only be accessed by registered retailers and check for acceptance of the sales agreement and completion of product payments. If these conditions are met, the contract performs the transaction that the distributor delivers the product to the retailer. The contract status changes to *SaleRequestAgreedSuccess*, the distributor status changes to *ProductSoldToRetailer*, and the retailer status changes to *ProductDeliveredSuccessful*. Otherwise, for failures, the contract status changes to *SaleRequestDenied*, the distributor status changes to *RequestFailed*, the retailer status changes to *ProductDeliveryFailure*.

Algorithm 2 Distributor Ships Product to Retailer

Input: *'r' is the list of registered Retailers*

    Etherenumaddress(EA) of Distributor, Etherenumaddress(EA) of Retailer,

    DateManufactured, Quantity Sold, DatePurchased

1 Contractstate is ***ProductSoldToDistributor***

2 Distributor state is ***ProductReceivedFromManufacturer***

3 i Retailer state is ***ReadyToPurchase***

4 Restrict access to only r retailer

5 if *Sale = agreed and ProductPayment = successful* **then**

6   Contract state changes to *SaleRequestAgreedSuccess.*

7   Distributor state changes to *ProductSoldToRetailer.*

8   Retailer state is *ProductDeliveredSuccessful*

9   Create a 'success' notification message.

10 end

11 else

12   Contract state changes to *SaleRequestDenied.*

13   Distributor state changes to *RequestFailed.*

14   Retailer state is *ProductDeliveryFailure*

15   is Create a request failure notification message.

16 end

17 else

18   Revert contract state and show an error.

19 end

---

5 Traceability Scheme Performance Analysis

Table 1 shows the gas value consumed by different nodes when they call the smart contract to trade after deploying the smart contract to the block chain, and the corresponding ether consumption in the Ethernet. From Table 1, it can be seen that users only need to spend very little ether when making transaction requests on the chain, and the transaction costs will not cause losses to the interests of the nodes, so it is implementable.

Table 1. Transaction consumption.

Transaction type	Consumption (gas)	Consumption (ETH)
updateProductInformation()	21272	0.000021
sellProductInformation()	23896	0.000024
buyProductFromMfacturer()	26264	0.000026
sellProductToRetailer()	25048	0.000025
buyProductFromDistributor()	21271	0.000021
sellEndProduct()	21272	0.000021

In Table 2, we compare the performance of the intelligent contract designed in this paper with that of Xu's [5] data reading delay in the paper, the time unit is milliseconds. From Table 2, we can see that because the block chain data is read locally but not sent to the block chain network, the data can be read quickly. Compared with Xu's scheme, the smart contract data read latency designed in this paper is lower and the performance is a little better.

Table 2. Reading latency(ms).

	Xu's scheme	Mine
Minimum	8	6
Fist quartile	10	12
Median	11	1
Third quartile	13	10
Maximum	129	120
Average	17	13

6 Conclusion

In this article, we first introduced the difficulties and challenges of current mainstream food traceability program. Then, through in-depth analysis of the main needs of users, we designed a food traceability scheme based on blockchain and EPC technology. To alleviate the data explosion problem, we used collaborative management of on- and-off-chain data to reduce the amount of data for a single node. Constructed a smart contract module for trading on chain to ensure the security and effectiveness of node transactions. The experiment proved that the intelligent contract designed in this paper had good performance and was implementable.

References

1. Fors, E., Thankur, M., Solem, K., Svarva, R.: State of traceability in the Norwegian food sectors. Food Control 62–69 (2015). https://doi.org/10.1016/j.foodcont.2015.03.027
2. Ricardo, B.M., Mishra, P., Ruiz-Garcíaa, L.: Food traceability: new trends and recent advances. A review. Food Control 393–401 (2015). https://doi.org/10.1016/j.foodcont.2015.05.005
3. Distributed ledger technology: beyond blockchain. Technical report, UK Government Chief Scientific Adviser (2016)
4. Staples, M., Chen, S., Falamaki, S., Ponomarev, A., Rimba, P.: Risks and opportunities for systems using blockchain and smart contracts. Technical report, Sydney, Data61(CSIRO) (2017). https://doi.org/10.1007/978-3-030-16184-2
5. Xu, X., Liu, Q., Liu, Y., Zhu, L., Yao, H., Vasilakosd, A.V.: Designing blockchain-based applications a case study for imported product traceability. Future Gener. Comput. Syst. 399–406 (2019). https://doi.org/10.1016/j.future.2018.10.010
6. Abeyratne, S.A., Monfared, R.: Blockchain ready manufacturing supply chain using distributed ledger. Int. J. Res. Eng. Technol. **05**(09), 1–10 (2016)
7. Niya, S.R., Dordevic, D., Nabi, A.G., Mann, T., Stiller, B.: A platform-independent, generic-purpose, and blockchain-based supply chain tracking. In: 2019 IEEE International Conference on Blockchain and Cryptocurrency (ICBC), pp. 14–17. IEEE (2019)
8. Toyoda, K., Mathiopoulos, P.T., Sasase, I., Ohtsuki, T.: A novel blockchain-based Product Ownership Management System (POMS) for anti-counterfeits in the post supply chain. IEEE Access 1 (2017). https://doi.org/10.1109/ACCESS.2017.2720760
9. Tian, F.: An agri-food supply chain traceability system for China based on RFID & blockchain technology. In: 2016 13th International Conference on Service Systems and Service Management (ICSSSM), pp. 1–8. IEEE (2016). https://doi.org/10.1109/ICICTA.2009.700
10. Zyskind, G., Nathan, O., Alex: Decentralizing privacy: using blockchain to protect personal data. In: 2015 IEEE Security and Privacy Workshops (SPW). IEEE Computer Society (2015). https://doi.org/10.1109/SPW.2015.27
11. Zhu, L., Wu, Y., Gai, K., Choo, K.K.R.: Controllable and trustworthy blockchain-based cloud data management. Future Gener. Comput. Syst. **91**, 527–535 (2019)
12. Gai, K., Wu, Y., Zhu, L., Qiu, M., Shen, M.: Privacy-preserving energy trading using consortium blockchain in smart grid. IEEE Trans. Ind. Inform. **15**, 3548–3558 (2019)
13. Gai, K., Wu, Y., Zhu, L., Xu, L.: Permissioned blockchain and edge computing empowered privacy-preserving smart grid networks. IEEE Internet Things J. 1 (2019)
14. Wang, S.: Internet of things based on EPC technology and its application in logistics. In: 2011 2nd International Conference on Artificial Intelligence, Management Science and Electronic Commerce (AIMSEC). IEEE (2011). https://doi.org/10.1109/AIMSEC.2011.6010861

15. Nizamuddin, N., Salah, K., Ajmal-Azad, M., Arshad, J., Rehman, M.H.: Decentralized document version control using ethereum blockchain and IPFS. Comput. Electr. Eng. **76**, 183–197 (2019)
16. Bahga, A., Vijay, K., Madisetti, A.: Next-generation smart contract and decentralized application platform. J. Softw. Eng. Appl. (2016)
17. Nakamoto, S.: Bitcoin: a peer-to-peer electronic cash system. Consulted (2008)

Towards Blockchain-Based Auditing
of Data Exchanges

Xiaohu Zhou, Antonio Nehme, Vitor Jesus$^{(\boxtimes)}$, Yonghao Wang,
Mark Josephs, and Khaled Mahbub

School of Computing and Digital Technology, Birmingham City University,
Birmingham B4 7XG, UK
Xiaohu.zhou@mail.bcu.ac.uk,
{antonio.nehme,vitor.jesus,yonghao.wang,
mark.josephs,Khaled.Mahbub}@bcu.ac.uk

Abstract. Auditing operations in multi-party data exchange, and over an arbitrary topology, is a common requirement yet still an open problem especially in the case where no trust on any participating party can be presumed. The challenges range from storage of the audit trail to tampering and collusion of participating entities. In this paper, we propose a blockchain-based auditing scheme. It is designed based on public key infrastructure and Shamir secret sharing scheme.

Keywords: Blockchain · Data share · Auditable · Smart-contracts

1 Introduction

Controlling how sensitive data is shared is an open problem with no complete solution in sight. Beyond the impact of the loss of data itself, it also brings a sharp negative impact on the public's trust and discourage them to engage with electronic systems or share their data [1]. Auditing of workflow is thus a key element when handling data flows. Considering a simple supply chain scenario in Fig. 1, which involves a customer (C), a sales company (S), a manufacturer (M), and a logistics organization (L). When C places an order with S, S receives the order and then sends the product requirements to M. M produces the goods after the received requirements and asks L to deliver the product to C within the agreed upon timeframe. Then C receives the goods from L. Let's assume C is not satisfied with the product due to a defect and needs to return it. The key issue is which entity is responsible for this error. L may be responsible for the fault because of a failure in handling the package or M may have given a defective product to the delivery company. If no companies admit the error, and all parties produce their own internal records showing no fault, one can only assume some of them intentionally modified the existing records in their system to prevent truthful auditing. Having a robust audit system with immutable audit trail is vital to assure non-repudiation and assign accountability for malpractice [2].

© Springer Nature Switzerland AG 2019
M. Qiu (Ed.): SmartBlock 2019, LNCS 11911, pp. 43–52, 2019.
https://doi.org/10.1007/978-3-030-34083-4_5

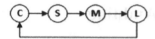   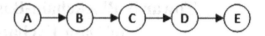

Fig. 1. An example scenario   **Fig. 2.** A representation of a data exchange workflow

Blockchain is a decentralized distributed ledger that contains an ordered list of records in a chain [3]. It is a promising innovation technique given its intrinsic distribution and immutability properties having found application in both financial and non-financial areas [4, 5], such as government public management [5], healthcare industry [6, 7], and privacy preserving in data sharing networks [8, 9]. Blockchain also enables a peer-to-peer transactions without intermediaries or trust relationship agreement.

In this paper, we propose a novel scheme to construct tamper-resisted audit trails by leveraging the blockchain technology. We also provide a theoretical support of data exchange in the confidentiality and accountability. In the reminder of this paper, Sect. 2 reviews related work and Sect. 3 formulates our problem. Section 4 proposes our approach and implementation is discussed in Sect. 5. Section 6 concludes our paper.

2 Related Work

Research in blockchain is covered in diverse domains most notably aspects of traceability and immutability, such as auditing workflow in government processes [10], enterprise business [11], and healthcare data exchange [12, 13]. For government applications, permissionless blockchain is not considered to be suitable for government audit systems due to the difficulty of verifying user identities and enforcing strict data governance [10].

Some prior work give a literature review of blockchain technology in auditing environment [10, 14], which provided a theoretical support without empirical practice. Blockchain technology provides a solution to automate mechanism for trust without intermediary [10], such as any central authorities. It can also be used to minimize fraud, optimize the existing procedures, and reduce workloads of auditors [14]. However, those papers have not mentioned more details on how to integrate the blockchain technology with the existing auditing processes.

In the prototype design, many previous researches have involved in the proof of concepts development with blockchain. To audit transactions in the data exchange workflow, Ahmad et al. propose a system that records distributed and immutable logs in the Hyperledger blockchain against the external and internal attacks [11]. The transparent logs are stored in the public blockchain without access restrictions. Therefore, this system is not suitable for credential authorities or institutions that require secrecy. Pourmajidi et al. [15] propose an approach based on the super-blockchain and circled blockchain to record and receive logs. Individuals can access logs through some APIs to the immutable hierarchical ledger. The key issue is that this scheme may increase the time to retrieve logs because of the multiple-hierarchical structure of blocks storage. An evaluation is required to verify the impact their proposal on performance. Suzuki et al. design a prototype system based upon the test environment of Bitcoin [16], which is to use blockchain to construct audit logs for strictly access controlled in client-server communication channel. It cannot solve the high-energy consumption as well as the latency in system implementation caused by the mining process, although there is compensated through coin returns.

3 Problem Statement

This section formulates the problems that we tackle, presents a threat model, and lists the designed goals.

3.1 Problem Definition

To illustrate, we use a linear topology - see Fig. 2. Nodes (A, B–E) represent the involved organisations or individuals that they are objects to transmit data. The arrow represents the direction of data flow. The processes of data flow and the related entities are pre-established, which means the interaction between workflow participants are pre-defined. When A is the information sender, who wants to send information to B. A knows the receiver is B and B knows the sender is A. If an outside attacker plants a forged data instead of the payload that B sent to C, we need to ensure that the honest node C can detect this action. If B colludes with D that they tamper with the existing audit information and repudiate performed actions to avoid incrimination during inspection, there should be enough evidence to make other honest nodes spot the incorrect data. If a confidential data is exfiltrated, it is necessary to ensure that the data is encrypted and exposed minimal information. This paper focuses on the level of security improvement in aspects of the accountability of data exchange and transactions reflecting performed actions of the involved participants. We propose a blockchain-based smart auditable check scheme to solve problems that mentioned above.

3.2 Threats Model and Assumptions

In this section, we present out threat model and security assumptions. The audit server includes codes of a smart-contract run on the blockchain that is trusted to perform the protocol, which stores audit records and conducts the verification triggered by the workflow participants. The workflow participants are trusted but some of them may collude with others to intentionally deny their mischievous actions or modify the existing information in the storage after the fact. The outside attackers can eavesdrop on message from the transmission channel and plant forged message instead of the true one in the workflow. Any of participants in the workflow can collude with others to repudiate the performed actions. Therefore, we propose a scheme that is based upon assumptions as below:

Assumption 1: the blockchain is deemed as trusted to immutable store data.
Assumption 2: the workflow participants do not intentionally expose their private keys.
Assumption 3: there is at least one honest participant in every workflow.

3.3 Designed Goals

We design our proposed scheme to satisfy the following goals:

- Confidentiality and integrity. All workflow participants cannot forge or tamper the existing information after-the-fact. Only the data owner can generate correct encrypted audit logs. The nodes of blockchain and workflow cannot forge or tamper the audit logs even if they are dishonest individuals or collude with others. Besides, the audit logs are only stored and verified in cipher form. They cannot be exposed intentionally in a plaintext form. In other words, they cannot be viewed or modified in an undetected or unauthorized way. What's more, the audit server is only store the related encrypted audit logs and keys.
- Availability. Participants cannot escape the audit processes when they require a service. All encrypted audit logs are tamper-resistant and stored in the blockchain. The honest node can access the audit trail to verify the received data.

The above security aspects help to achieve accountability assurance that enabled by having reliable evidence. Our security model renders our approach suitable for applications in which the confidentiality of digital evidence is a requirement. We also aim to assure the availability and integrity of audit trails.

4 Proposed Approach

Our proposed scheme relies on public key cryptography (PKI), a group of signatures, records verification, and Shamir secret sharing scheme. PKI is used to encrypt exchanged messages which improves the confidentiality of workflow. Shamir secret scheme has a positive impact on the protection of encrypted data (in our case is the audit trail). It is theoretically not feasible to decrypt the audit records with one split of the key [17]. The usage of a group of signatures is to mark each action that ensures the data integrity. Audit records verification is an important component, which enables participants to check the correctness of audit records equivalent to a transaction that was received. In this section, we introduce the description of notation, system architecture, the related protocol, and key management.

4.1 Notation

For easier of description and reference, symbols used in the proposed scheme are summarized as below (Table 1). The keyGen is an abbreviation of key generation.

Table 1. A table of notation description

Symbols	Descriptions
N	$N \in n$, $n = \{1 \ldots m\}$. n is a set of nodes that includes many (m) nodes in a workflow, N presents one node
WK, WSK	A public and private keys of each workflow
K_a	A split Shamir key of WSK for a single node
PK_N	A public key of a single node
SK_N	A secrete private key of a single node
M_{NM}	A plaintext message sent from node N to M
E_N, E_{WK}	A message encrypted with PK_N of N, or WK of workflow
S_N	A message signed by node N
$Payload_{NM}$	A processed message sent from node N to M
$Notice_{NM}$	A feedback of payload received from node N to M
$SysLog_{NM}$	A system log records operation of node N for M
$AudLog_{NM}$	An audit log contains hash value of the related system log

4.2 System Architecture

We show a view of the system architecture of our proposed scheme (see Fig. 3), which includes three main components: nodes, audit server, and certificate authority.

- Nodes. They are participants involved in the workflow, such as authorities, stakeholders, and so on. In this paper, each node represents one of entities that collaborates and exchanges information in a workflow.
- Audit server. We run the audit server in the Ethereum blockchain. All audit trails are encrypted and then stored in the blockchain that can be accessed by nodes.
- Certificate authority (CA). It is a trusted authority to generate keys for diverse workflows. This can be a professional authority that depends on the workflow.

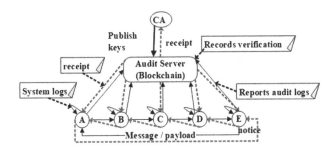

Fig. 3. The system architecture of the proposed scheme

4.3 Key Management

We assume that all entities have a unique identification and it can be used in the different workflows. Each workflow has a specified single pair of keys that can be only used in this workflow.

- Identity key management. To identify all relevant participants, all of them have their unique pair of keys when they register in the blockchain. Every public key is stored in the blockchain. Participants save their private keys as identities and use them to approve transaction in the workflow.
- Workflow key management. A CA provides a unique single pair of keys for every workflow. The private key of the workflow is divided into pieces of partial keys based upon the cryptographic algorithm of Shamir's secret sharing [17]. The amount of Shamir threshold keys depends on numbers of participants in the workflow. Every participant has its own part of *WSK* for each workflow. At the same time, the CA stores all workflow public keys to the blockchain.

4.4 Protocol

We show a protocol to implement our auditable check scheme in this section. It is composed of three phases, which are system initialization, data exchange, and records verification. Figure 4 shows a part of sequence diagram of the proposed protocol.

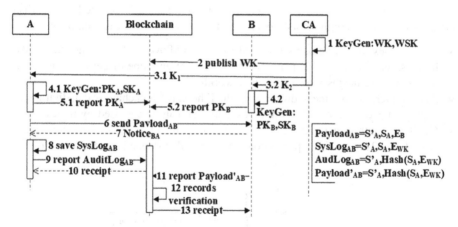

Fig. 4. A sequence diagram of our scheme. The initial phase (step 1–5) is key generation and distribution. Phase 2 (step 6–10) is data processes between participant and blockchain. Phase 3 (step 11–13) is records verification.

Phase 1: System Initialization. It aims to initialize keys of the participants and workflow. All participants have a cryptographic key pair (PK_N and SK_N) as their identities. A CA provides a single pair of keys for each workflow (WK and WSK). Each node has a public key (WK) and a split of the private key (K_n) of each workflow. In the Fig. 4, A has PK_A, SK_A, WK, and K_I. The blockchain stores keys of PK_A and WK.

Phase 2: Data Exchange. In this phase, the message sender signs and encrypts the predefined message to ensure the security of transmission. When A wants to send message to B, the initial payload is M_{AB}. First, A needs to sign M_{AB} and then encrypt it with key PK_B of B. The payload is represented by

$$Payload_{AB} = Encrypt_B[Sign_A(M_{AB}) + M_{AB}] = (S_A, E_B) \tag{1}$$

Then, A signs the encrypted payload again to mark the previous performed action before the payload transmission. The payload is expressed by

$$Payload_{AB} = Sign'_A(Payload_{AB}) + Payload_{AB} = (S'_A, S_A, E_B) \tag{2}$$

During the date exchange, a system log is generated to record the exchanged data. Each node stores their system logs in the local storage. The hash values of these system logs (namely, *audit log*) are published timely to the audit server as the immutable blocks. A system log includes an encrypted message with a key *WK* and a group of signatures. The second signature is to verify that encrypted logs have not been tampered with without having to decrypt the logs. When an audit log is saved in the blockchain, the message sender receives a receipt from the scheme. In the Fig. 4, $SysLog_{AB}$ is the system log that records the data exchange between A and B. $AudLog_{AB}$ is the published audit log to the blockchain for the audit trail. They are represented respectively by

$$SysLog_{AB} = Sign'_A[Encrypt_{WK}(Sign_A, M_{AB})] + Encrypt_{WK}(Sign_A, M_{AB}) \tag{3}$$

$$AudLog_{AB} = [S'_A, Hash(S_A, E_{WK})] \tag{4}$$

Phase 3: Records Verification. This phase is to verify all performed actions of data flow from workflow participants. The participant always checks whether the hash value of encrypted payload ($Payload'_{NM}$) is matched with audit log ($AudLog_{NM}$). When the recipient received the payload ($Payload_{NM}$) from the sender, the cipher message (M_{NM}) is decrypted with a private key (SK_N) of the recipient. Before the match, M_{NM} is encrypted again with a workflow public key (*WK*) by the recipient and conducted as a new payload ($Payload'_{NM}$). Then, it is the comparison of the hash value of $Payload'_{NM}$ and $AudLog_{NM}$ in a smart-contract. If the result of match is false, the workflow is stopped. Considering the integrity of data in the flow, the recipient needs to give a feedback ($Notice_{NM}$) to the sender when the payload is transferred. For example, when B receives payload from A successfully, a notice is sent to A.

Then, B gets the M_{AB} from the payload through the decryption of the $Payload_{AB}$ with key S_{KB}. In the match, B encrypts M_{AB} with key *WK* and calculates a hash value of it. The new payload is represented by

$$Payload'_{AB} = [S'_A, S_A, Hash(E_{WK})] \tag{5}$$

5 Performance Evaluation

We implement our scheme in the Ethereum blockchain, with the blockchain as the audit server that is conducted in a smart-contract for the data verification and audit log storage. We design a simple user interface as the interaction client for the workflow participant, which is to report and download audit log, and trigger with the smart-contract. The following context is also to analyze how the scheme achieves the security requirements.

5.1 Implementation

The implementation of our scheme is mainly to build codes of smart-contracts. Figure 5 shows a representative smart-contract code. There are two smart-contracts to enable the records verification and audit logs reporting. First contract 'AuditLog' constructs a function 'generateLog' to save audit trail into the blockchain as the immutable storage. Second contract 'Verification' is an inheritance contract of the first one, it is developed to access audit trail from the blockchain and verify the records. The function 'getLog' is to get audit trail by the specified address, notably, the account address of audit log reporter. The function 'compareLogs' is to compare hash values of audit trail and payload. This function is required to only operate by the current account of participant. 'ownerOf' function is a modifier to implement the operation control for function 'compareLogs'. When a node performs the data transmission in the workflow, a new contract will be created to save audit log into the blockchain. Once a node receives a payload from the previous node, the node can verify the payload through the smart-contract.

```
Contract AuditLog {
    string hashOfMessage;
    string signature;
    event NewLog(uint logId, string signature, string hash);
    struct Log { string signature; string hash; }
    Log[] public logs;
    Mapping (uint => address) public logOwner;
    function generateLog(string _signature, string_hash)
        internal returns (bool) {
        _hash = hashOfMessage;
        _signature = signature;
        uint id = logs.push(Log(_signature, _hash)) – 1;
        logOwner[id] = msg.sender;
        NewLog(id, _signature, _hash);
        return true;
    }}
Contract Verification is AuditLog {
    mapping (address => string) previousLog;
    modifier ownerOf(uint _logId) {
        require(msg.sender == logOwner[_logId];
        _;
    }
    function getLog (address _myAddress) public view returns(string) {
        return previousLog[_myAddress];
    }
    function compareLogs(uint _presentId, uint _targetId)
        public view ownerOf(_presentId) returns (bool) {
        Log storage presentLog = logs[_presentId];
        Log storage targetLog = logs[_targetId];
        if (keccak256(abi.encodePacked(presentLog.hash))
            == keccak256(abi.encodePacked(targetLog.hash)) )
        { return true; } else { return false; }
    }}
```

Fig. 5. The central smart-contract. One contract is to generate a new block to save the audit log with function 'generateLog'. The second one is an inheritance of the first one that verifies the data from audit log and payload, which consists of function 'getLog' and 'compareLogs'.

5.2   Security Analysis

We discuss the security requirements for the proposed scheme in malicious operations as below. It includes malicious participant and collusion attacks.

Malicious Participant. In a workflow, a dishonest entity can eavesdrop data from the transmission channel, disrupt the data flow, or plant a forged message into the flow. However, the honest entity can detect these attacks with the audit record verification mechanism in the proposed scheme. We discuss internal and external aspects of malicious attacks. For the internal attacks, if an internal node tries to withhold a payload to interrupt the data exchange, the next node cannot receive the related payload. Therefore, this malicious attempt is detected on the fly. If the internal node uses the fraudulent data instead of the original payload, it can be detected in the records verification. There is an error when the hash value of the fake payload matches with the original one in the audit log. If the node tampers with or removes a local audit record, records on the audit server will reveal the malicious activities because of the immutability of blockchain. As for the external attacks, based on the assumption 2 and without the knowledge of participants' private keys, the external node cannot plant a forged message to pass the verification. The honest node can detect the attempt. In addition, the message are exchanged in encrypted form, it makes eavesdropping on the data flow useless to external attacks.

Collusion Attacks. When two or more than two nodes collude with each other in the data flow, their fraudulent actions can be exposed by the honest node (assumption 3). For instance, we assume that B colludes with C in Fig. 3. When D receives the forged payload ($Payload_{CD}$) from C, the hash value comparison between $Payload_{CD}$ with $AudLog_{CD}$ is triggered by D. If there is not match in the comparison, C is suspected of that malicious behavior. What's more, even if C repudiates it and ask B to frame A, we can verify $AudLog_{AB}$ and $Payload_{AB}$ to against it. If B colludes with D, they plant forged payloads ($Payload_{BC}$, $Payload_{DA}$) and deny their performed actions. For this case, the honest node can also detect it. C and A can verify payloads separately when they receive payload. As seen, our proposed protocol mitigates the impact of collusion attacks as possible.

6   Conclusion

In this paper, we discussed the usage of the Ethereum blockchain to enable auditing of workflow transactions. We provided a blockchain-based smart auditable check scheme that constructs a complete immutable audit trail for every action of participants in data transmission. Our audit scheme satisfies our aim to enable confidentiality, integrity, and accountability for a generic topology of data flow. As for future work, we will test the scheme in the real Ethereum network. The latency of new block generated is a consideration that affects the data flow efficiency. Besides, the generation of key pair for each workflow is also concern due to human factors from the certification authority. Furthermore, the security and stability of smart-contract need to be analyzed.

References

1. Reddick, C., Anthopoulos, L.: Interactions with e-government, new digital media and traditional channel choices: citizen-initiated factors. Transform. Gov. People Process. Policy **8**(3), 398–419 (2014)
2. Nehme, A., Jesus, V., Mahbub, K., Abdallah, A.: Decentralised and collaborative auditing of workflows. In: 16th International Conference on Trust, Privacy and Security in Digital Business (2019)
3. Esposito, C., De Santis, A., Tortora, G., Chang, H., Choo, K.K.R.: Blockchain: a panacea for healthcare cloud-based data security and privacy? IEEE Cloud Comput. **5**, 31–37 (2018)
4. Crosby, M., Pattanayak, P., Verman, S., Kalyanaraman, V.: Blockchain technology: beyond bitcoin. Appl. Innov. Rev. **2**(6–19), 71 (2016)
5. Nofer, M., Gomber, P., Hinz, O., Schiereck, D.: Blockchain. Bus. Inf. Syst. Eng. **59**(3), 183–187 (2017)
6. Guo, R., Shi, H., Zhao, Q., Zheng, D.: Secure attribute-based signature scheme with multiple authorities for blockchain in electronic health records systems. IEEE Access **6**, 11676–11686 (2018)
7. Li, H., Fan, K., Yang, Y., Ren, Y., Wang, S.: MedBlock: efficient and secure medical data sharing via blockchain. J. Med. Syst. **42**, 136 (2018)
8. Gai, K., Wu, Y., Zhu, L., Qiu, M., Shen, M.: Privacy-preserving energy trading using consortium blockchain in smart grid. IEEE Trans. Industr. Inf. **15**(6), 3548–3558 (2019)
9. Gai, K., Wu, Y., Zhu, L., Xu, L., Zhang, Y.: Permissioned blockchain and edge computing empowered privacy-preserving smart grid networks. IEEE Internet Things J.
10. Antipova, T.: Using blockchain technology for government auditing. In: Iberian Conference on Information Systems and Technologies, CISTI, pp. 1–6 (2018)
11. Ahmad, A., Saad, M., Bassiouni, M., Mohaisen, A.: Towards blockchain-driven, secure and transparent audit logs. In: 15th EAI International Conference on Mobile and Ubiquitous Systems: Computing, Networking and Services, pp. 443–448 (2018)
12. Castaldo, L., Cinque, V.: Blockchain-based logging for the cross-border exchange of eHealth data in Europe. In: Gelenbe, E., et al. (eds.) Euro-CYBERSEC 2018. CCIS, vol. 821, pp. 46–56. Springer, Cham (2018). https://doi.org/10.1007/978-3-319-95189-8_5
13. Anderson, J.: Record Audit Logs Through Permissioned Blockchain Technology (2018)
14. Abreu, P.W., Aparicio, M., Costa, C.J.: Blockchain technology in the auditing environment. In: Iberian Conference on Information Systems and Technologies, CISTI, pp. 1–6 (2018)
15. Pourmajidi, W., Miranskyy, A.: Logchain: blockchain-assisted log storage. In: IEEE International Conference on Cloud Computing, CLOUD, pp. 978–982 (2018)
16. Suzuki, S., Murai, J.: Blockchain as an audit-able communication channel. In: IEEE 41st Annual International Computer Software and Applications Conference, vol. 2, pp. 516–522 (2017)
17. Shamir, A.: How to share a secret. Commun. ACM **22**, 612–613 (1979)

Feasibility of Stellar as a Blockchain-Based Micropayment System

Nida Khan[1]([⊠])⬤, Tabrez Ahmad[2]⬤, and Radu State[1]⬤

[1] University of Luxembourg,
29, Avenue JF Kennedy, 8358 Luxembourg, Luxembourg
nida.khan@uni.lu
[2] ArcelorMittal, 24-26, Bd Avaranches, 1160 Luxembourg, Luxembourg

Abstract. The advent of Bitcoin was heralded as an innovation in the global monetary system, that could bring down transaction fees by circumventing the need for third parties and conduct transactions in real time. The divisibility of a blockchain cryptocurrency to even fractions of a cent, caused microtransactions to become feasible to formerly non-existent denominations. These microtransactions have spurred the development of novel ways of monetizing online resources and hold the potential to aid in alleviation of poverty. The paper conducts a feasibility study on Stellar as a blockchain-based micropayment system. It highlights the limitations in Stellar that impedes its progress and utilizes a characterization model for micropayment systems to evaluate the efficacy of the Stellar platform. The paper conducts a comparison with the micropayment solutions from Bitcoin, Ethereum and PayPal. The paper analyzes a subset of transactions from the Stellar blockchain to aid in drawing a conclusion on the undertaken study and elaborates on the mitigation tools to enable fraud prevention in online monetary transactions.

Keywords: Blockchain · Micropayments · Stellar · Data analysis · Cybercrime

1 Introduction

Stellar is a public blockchain-based payment network, that connects financial organizations and people to provide extremely low cost, cross-border payment transfers within seconds. Stellar was released in April 2015 by the Stellar Development Foundation and was initially brought into conception in 2014 by McCaleb and Kim. The blockchain platform came into inception with the mission to increase access to low cost financial services, to reduce poverty and maximize individual potential. Stellar expounds the facility of smaller payment transfers, micropayments, with an increased efficiency. Tempo, a payment system, utilizes Stellar to send remittances from Europe to the world and 600000 transactions can be executed incurring a $0.01 fee, making Stellar blockchain a very good candidate for micropayment systems [1].

The high cost associated with financial transaction fees, whether it is through an online bank transfer or the use of a card service led to the need of demarcation of online payments of low value to be in another category of payments, namely micropayments, whereby they could be dealt with in a different way to leverage lower transaction fees.

M. Qiu (Ed.): SmartBlock 2019, LNCS 11911, pp. 53–65, 2019.
https://doi.org/10.1007/978-3-030-34083-4_6

Micropayment systems are electronic payment systems, which facilitate a payment transaction of a dollar or less but there is no defined threshold [2, 3]. Presently, companies like PayPal, Apple and even Starbucks are attempting to provide micropayments to address a demand for payments of small amounts to indulge in purchases for online games, web content, online advertising and website usage. Micropayments also provide a mechanism to protect the intellectual property rights of owners of digital content to ensure payment to access their content. Micropayment systems provide an alternative means of monetizing digital services for revenue generation in contrast to using online advertising and selling private data of consumers. Digital giants like Facebook employ a mechanism of generating revenue through advertising by compromising on users' privacy and recorded a revenue of $16.91 billion in the last quarter of December 2018 [4]. The monthly and annual subscription models to generate revenue through online media is turning out to be infeasible with many media outlets resorting to layoffs [5]. This has led to a resurgence of interest in cryptocurrency micropayments.

Blockchain absolves the need to trust intermediaries in financial transactions, reducing both transaction time and cost, making the technology suitable for micropayment transactions. Bitcoin was plagued with scalability issues leading to the development of Lightning Network for off-chain, low cost and nearly instant payments, including micropayments [6]. The high transaction fee of Bitcoin transactions failed to bring micropayments into everyday use. Similarly, Ethereum developed Raiden on state channel technology to provide micropayments in ERC20 tokens [7]. Other initiatives catering to providing means for web monetization include novel ventures like Facebook's Libra [8], Mozilla's Brave browser [9] and Coil [10] amongst others.

This paper conducts a feasibility study on Stellar as a blockchain-based micropayment system. The paper emphasizes the significance of blockchain-based micropayments and highlights the issues that are an obstruction to the optimum utilization of Stellar. The paper is a pioneer in assessing Stellar and related blockchain-based micropayment systems on the basis of a characterization model for micropayments. A theoretical study of Stellar is corroborated with empirical evidence from the data analysis of a subset of Stellar transactions to conclude on the feasibility of the blockchain network as a micropayment solution. The paper gives the motivation for this work in Sect. 2. Related work is discussed in Sect. 3. Section 4 gives a brief description of Stellar highlighting the network's drawbacks, while Sect. 5 presents a comparative listing of characteristics of Stellar as a micropayment system. Analysis of Stellar payment transactions is given in Sect. 6. Mitigation strategies in Stellar to prevent online fraud are given in Sect. 7 with the conclusion of the undertaken feasibility study given in Sect. 8.

2 Motivation

Numerous micropayment initiatives have mushroomed but are plagued with implementation issues like authentication of bank accounts and the requirement to constantly monitor the transaction fee incurred, impeding the development of reliable, secure, efficient and user-friendly micropayment systems, catering to less than $1. IBM and

Compaq attempted to develop their own micropayment platforms in 1999 and attempts were made to enable the World Wide Consortium to develop a standard to cater to seamless micropayment transactions in future through the Internet. Many other companies like Cybercoin, Millicent and Digicash, among others, started developing their own micropayment solutions. However, attempts towards the same were discarded for many reasons, including a lack of interest from consumers and overall infeasibility of such a platform without a definite profit margin [11]. The motivation for this work emerged from the search for a viable blockchain-based micropayment system, in consideration of the many application areas, as enumerated below:

- **Digital Content.** Blockchain-based micropayment systems can be used for *Prepaid* payment systems as well as *Pay-As-You-Go* models. Prepaid payment models cater to subscriptions based on a certain time duration to allow access to some product/service. Pay-As-You-Go models can be utilized to pay for reading content online, pay for access to Internet or buy products. They can be used to achieve an advertisement free experience of browsing the Internet, pay for watching movies, listening to music and reading news, books and other digital content.
- **Thing-to-Thing Micropayments.** Blockchain can be used in the energy sector with applications in smart grid networks [12, 13]. Internet of Things technology would benefit from the feature of devices being able to pay each other without any human interaction and blockchain-based micropayments can provide this feature to enable thing-to-thing payments. This would allow devices to pay other devices for using their computational power or pay for electricity usage [14].
- **Humanitarian Causes.** Donations have long been under scrutiny for lack of transparency and an evaluation of their impact on the disseminated money to those in need. Blockchain-based micropayments especially coupled with smart contracts can prove to be a panacea to solve the problems in the donation industry. Payments less than $1 can be transferred using blockchain solutions to cater to the needs of underdeveloped and developing countries in a transparent way, ensuring both the amount of the money reaching the needy as well as recording the impact [15].
- **Financial Systems.** Blockchain-based micropayments can be utilized to build customized crowdfunding and crowdlending platforms for small and medium enterprises as well as farmers, who lack access to the available financial services for reasons attributing to as belonging to low income groups, being geographically isolated and not utilizing the banking services for ethical reasons [16].
- **Social Causes.** Blockchain can be used to provide an identity system for immigrants and refugees, who fail to provide adequate paperwork for generation of conventional IDs. This can be achieved by using biometric identification mechanisms [17] with the blockchain-based micropayment systems providing daily wages and food vouchers.

3 Related Work

Micropayments have been an active area of research and much effort has gone into analyzing the efficacy of micropayment systems. Ali et al. did an exhaustive survey on the development of different micropayment systems [18]. Pass and Shelat proposed a new lottery-based micropayment scheme for ledger-based transaction systems [19]. Parhonyi et al. discuss the predictability of second-generation micropayment systems at faring better than the first generation systems by recognition of causative agents of failure in the first generation [20]. Lundqvist et al. propose a single fee micropayment protocol using blockchain technology [14]. Our previous work gives the economic impact of blockchain-based micropayment systems [16]. The present work involves a feasibility study of Stellar as a blockchain-based micropayment system, evaluating Stellar on a characterization model for micropayment systems, while highlighting the potential issues that impact its usage. The paper is a pioneer in analyzing the data of Stellar as a blockchain-based micropayment system.

4 Stellar

Stellar is an open-source, distributed, blockchain-based payments network that aids in the optimum conversion of fiat currency into cryptocurrency, lumens/XLM, to enable fast cross-border payments between different currencies at extremely reduced rates. The backbone of Stellar network is *Stellar Core*, supported by the *Horizon* API. Stellar is composed of multiple Stellar Cores with each owned by different people or organizations to ensure decentralization. Most applications interact with Stellar through Horizon, which provides the mechanism to submit transactions, check accounts and subscribe to events. The Stellar Cores work collaboratively as per the Stellar Consensus Protocol [21] to take a decision on the status of every transaction in the network.

The consensus mechanism used in Stellar is an implementation of Federated Byzantine Agreement (FBA), characterized by quorums and quorum slices. It is a generalization of Byzantine agreement to allow more settings like each node choosing it's own quorum slice. A quorum is defined as the set of nodes, that are sufficient to reach agreement. A quorum slice may entail a smaller number of nodes and be smaller than a quorum. FBA offers the functionality for each node to choose its quorum slice. A node may choose a quorum slice based on different criterion like reputation, financial reasons and tenure of participation in the network. Consensus in the entire network is reached based on the decisions of the individual quorum slices. FBA is supported by *Federated Voting*, which determines the vote of each node on a statement with the votes backed by the quorum slice of a node. Stellar supports smart contracts like Ethereum, though they are limited in functionality comparatively.

4.1 Methodology of Payments

Fiat money that is to be transferred in Stellar is first converted into XLM and then routed to the destination. Anchors in Stellar play the pivotal role of converting the fiat currency into cryptocurrency and serve as bridges between the users and the Stellar network (Fig. 1). These anchors need to be trustworthy and are generally banks and financial organizations. Stellar also provides a distributed currency exchange which gives the best exchange rate for a certain fiat currency. Stellar users need to have a certain minimum balance in their Stellar accounts before they can transfer money. Sending a payment is an operation in Stellar and a group of operations with additional information on the payer account and signature constitute a transaction. If one operation in a transaction fails, then all fail. Every operation has a base fee of 100 stroops, which is 0.00001 XLM. Stroop is the smallest unit of XLM. The transaction fee is determined by the base fee multiplied by the number of operations. It is independent of the payment amount and the number of hops in the payment route. An account can perform only one transaction at a time and every account has a sequence number, which helps to verify the order of transactions. The asset being sent through the payment needs to be specified. The native currency, XLM, other cryptocurrencies like BTC and fiat currencies like dollar for example, are permitted. In Stellar the amount of asset being sent is represented as a string to accommodate very small values and to do away with the inaccuracies introduced by floating point mathematics.

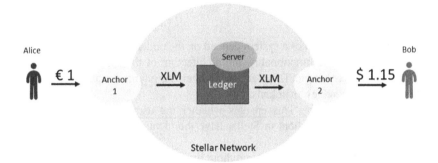

Fig. 1. Simplified view of a payment transfer in stellar

4.2 Issues and Limitations

Stellar blockchain platform suffers from some drawbacks, listed below, which limit its throughput and usage:

- Stellar depends on the need to trust anchors and thus, is not a true representative of a blockchain network, that upholds a distinguishing feature of absolving the need to trust intermediaries for conducting payments.
- Stellar charges even for those payments that fail to execute making the users pay for failed transactions. For example, a requirement in Stellar is to have a certain minimum number of XLM in each user account, without which a payment transfer would not go through. If a user sends a payment thereafter, it would fail with the user incurring fees [22].
- Stellar nodes have a transaction limit, thus restricting the throughput of the network. Transactions that are not included are held for a future ledger, when few transactions are waiting [1].

5 Characteristics of a Micropayment System

Academic literature on micropayment systems have suggested several characterization models for classifying and evaluating micropayment systems. Kniberg [23] presented a list of characteristics, while Abrazhevich [24] classified micropayment systems on the basis of user and technology-related characteristics. This paper uses the characterization model espoused by Weber [25], that classifies them into two groups, namely technical and non-technical. Micropayment systems have witnessed two phases of innovation [26], initiated by the emergence of the first generation in 1994, which failed by the end of 1990s. They were succeeded by the second generation systems in 1999–2000, with some of these persisting till today. The first generation systems concentrated on the technical characteristics of the systems, whereas the second generation focused on the non-technical characteristics. The discussion lists down most of the characteristics sufficient to help in reaching a conclusion on the undertaken study and a comparison is conducted in Table 1 between Stellar, Lightning Network, Raiden and PayPal to evaluate the feasibility of Stellar. A comparative review of the transaction fees of the concerned payment systems is given in [27].

5.1 Technical

The technical characteristics of a system depend on the underlying technology used and hence the focus is on the functionality and architecture of the systems under study.

1. *Medium of Exchange.* This defines whether the payment transfer is through a digital currency, fiat money or tokens.

2. *Anonymity of Users.* This ensures whether the user anonymity is preserved during transactions. The anchors in Stellar have the identity of the users and transactions can be traced back to them.

3. *Scalability.* This concerns the throughput limit of the blockchain platform. Stellar has integrated payment channels similar to Lightning Network to enhance it's scalability [28].

4. *Ease of Use.* This is an indication of the technical awareness needed to conduct a payment transfer by an average user.

5. *Validation.* This property determines whether an online contract with a third party is required for payment transfer.

6. *Security.* Security is evaluated here on the basis of payment delivery in the midst of fraud.

7. *Latency.* Micropayments should be conducted within a reasonable amount of time. The latency given in Table 1 for Lightning network and Raiden is for the use case where the payment channel needs to be opened and closed. Additionally in Raiden the token network contract needs to be deployed in Ethereum.

8. *Interoperability.* This implies users of one system can transfer a payment to another system in another currency.

5.2   Non-Technical

These characteristics deal with the usability of the system from the users' context.

9. *Privacy.* This deals with the availability of user data to third parties.

10. *Geographical Outreach.* This determines the geographical region within which the system can be used.

11. *Market Penetration.* This determines the total number of users of the system under study.

12. *Prepaid or Postpaid.* This indicates whether users need to deposit cryptocurrency before or after a payment transfer.

13. *Trust.* This deals with the confidence users have in the capability of the system, as well as to bearing of risks by the service provider. All risks are borne by the users in Stellar. For example if funds are stolen from the users account or en route a payment transfer, the liability would be with the user.

14. *Payment Threshold.* This defines the lower and upper bounds on the payments that can be conducted.

Table 1. Comparison of micropayment systems

Characteristics	Stellar	Lightning network	Raiden	PayPal
Medium of exchange	XLM	BTC	ERC20 tokens	25 fiat currencies
Anonymity	pseudonymous	anonymous	anonymous	pseudonymous
Scalability	1000+ tps[a] (1 billion users)	billions tps (envisaged)	billions tps (envisaged)	193 tps[b]
Ease of use	high technical knowledge	high technical knowledge	high technical knowledge	average technical knowledge
Validation	true	true (payment transfer through intermediaries)	true (payment transfer through intermediaries)	true
Security	public-key cryptography (*Ed25519*), offline storage of secret seed for generating public-private key pair	timelocks	Smart contracts and hashlocked payments	Information protected by SSL with a key length of 168 bits, stored on heavily guarded firewall-protected servers
Latency	3–5 s	1200+ s (*minimum*)	42+ s (*minimum*)	*withdrawal:* 0–72 h. *rest:* few minutes- 1 h.
Interoperability	yes for fiat and crypto	yes for blockchains with same hash function	allows atomic swaps with any ERC20 token	yes for fiat currencies

(continued)

Table 1. (*continued*)

Characteristics	Stellar	Lightning network	Raiden	PayPal
Privacy	anchors access data for regulatory compliance	payment information unavailable for offline transfers (*except for the initial and final transfer*), users known only by blockchain address	payment information unavailable for offline transfers (*except for the initial and final transfer*), users known only by blockchain address	third party has access to data
Geographical outreach	International	International	International	200 + countries/regions
Market penetration	1 million active user accounts in 3 years[c]	9102 nodes[d]	not available	277 million active accounts[e]
Prepaid/Postpaid	prepaid	prepaid	prepaid	prepaid, postpaid
Trust	low	low	low	high
Payment threshold	no limits	upper bound (restricted by channel capacity)	upper bound (restricted by channel capacity)	$10000/transaction[f]

a. Transactions per second.

b. Steemit, Transaction Speed – Bitcoin, Visa, Iota, PayPal https://steemit.com/cryptocurrency/@steemhoops99/transaction-speed-bitcoin-visa-iota-paypal

c. Jorn Van Zwanenburg. Stellar Achieves Milestone of 1 Million Active Accounts (2018). https://www.investinblockchain.com/stellar-1-million-accounts

d. Lightning Network Search and Analysis Engine (retrieved July 21, 2019).

e. Statista. https://www.statista.com/statistics/218493/paypals-total-active-registered-accounts-from-2010/

f. PayPal. https://www.paypal.com/lu/smarthelp/article/what-is-the-maximum-amount-i-can-send-with-my-paypal-account-faq732

6   Analysis of Stellar Payment Transactions

We analyzed 140,000 transaction records in Stellar, which involved some kind of asset transfer. The data, dates of transactions and scripts used can be accessed from the repository [29]. The reviewed data contained operations of the type '*payment*', '*path_payment*' and '*create_account*'. Payment operations, where the same asset is delivered to the receiver as sent by the payer, dominated and accounted for 98,282 transactions. Path payment operations, where the asset sent can differ from the one received, utilizing the decentralized exchange of Stellar, accounted for 5709 transactions. Operations 'create_account', which create and fund the account with the specified XLM, accounted for the remaining transaction records. We took micropayments to be less than/equal to US \$1 for our analysis with the exchange rates corresponding to the first quarter of 2019. It must be noted that the value of cryptocurrencies is volatile.

Figure 2 aids in achieving a waterfall analysis of the total payment transactions, where the major cryptocurrencies that dominated the transactions for payment transfers are indicated. The transactions in each listed cryptocurrency are further categorized into micropayment transfers and others. The listed cryptocurrencies, XLM, TXT, DRA, MFN and CMA accounted for 90.42% of the payment transactions, whereas all other cryptocurrencies accounted for the remaining. Among the 90.42% of the payment transactions, 83% were in the category of micropayments.

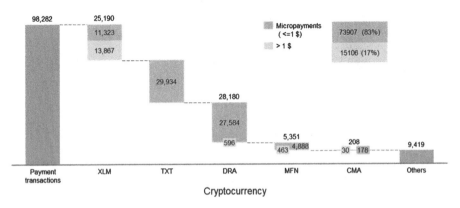

Fig. 2. Depiction of micropayment transactions in stellar payments with the cryptocurrency

Figure 3 depicts the payment transactions, grouped into major fee categories, in decreasing order. The figure also shows variation in the payment amounts with the transaction fee incurred and lists down the variation for 74.1% of the analyzed '*payment*' transaction records. It is observed that most of the payment transactions fall in the category of micropayments, in all the categories of transaction fee depicted. A major reason for this might be that most of the payment transactions, as seen in Fig. 2, were conducted using cryptocurrencies, whose exchange rates in USD were low at the time of computation. It is observed that both low and high transaction fee categories are composed majorly of micropayments. Stellar transaction fee is independent of the payment amount but increases with the increase in transaction complexity, measured by the number of operations in the transaction. Both simple and complex transactions constitute micropayments in payment transactions with the incurred transaction fees less than a cent.

Figure 4 depicts the major transaction fee categories, that were paid for 76.4% of the analyzed '*path_payment*' records. The number of transactions conducted, incurring that particular fee amount, are indicated alongside. It can be observed that a transaction fee of 100 stroops had 50% of the transactions in the category of micropayments, a fee of 200 stroops had 40% and a fee of 5216 stroops had only 10%. A higher transaction fee of 8000 stroops had no micropayment transactions. It can be concluded that micropayment transactions in path payments are less in complexity in terms of the number of operations.

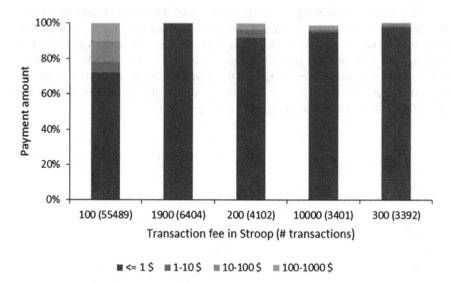

Fig. 3. Payment transactions - variation of transaction amounts in major fee categories

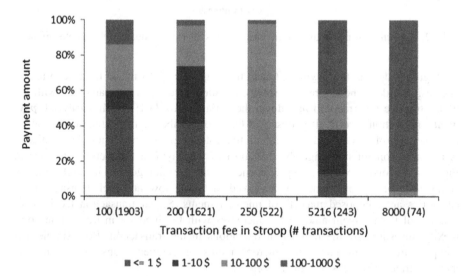

Fig. 4. Path payment transactions - variation of transaction amounts in major fee categories

7 Mitigation Strategy for Fraud Circumvention

The increasing dependence of the society on electronic communication networks has generated a new revenue stream for criminals, manifested in the cybercrime economy [30]. There is evidence that cybercrime revenues often exceed those of legitimate companies, with an annual revenue of at least $1.5 trillion [31]. Cryptocurrencies have been used as a medium of exchange majorly in dark markets, where Stellar and other blockchain-based micropayment systems can potentially be used for cybercrimes. Cryptocurrencies account for 4% of the money laundered and Bitcoin is considered to be an entrée to a far more developed world of money laundering [31], which utilizes an ever increasing group of emerging cryptocurrencies. Stellar provides support for regulatory compliance and Anti-Money laundering/Know Your Customer (AML/KYC) procedures through integration of the Federation and the Compliance Protocol [32]. The Federation protocol enables a mapping between user account addresses on Stellar to more information about the users. The Compliance protocol is an additional protocol that can optionally be used with the Federation protocol to facilitate exchange of AML information. A pre-built compliance service is provided that facilitates Compliance protocol requests to other organizations.

8 Conclusion

The study of Stellar indicates that it facilitates payments in seconds and is energy efficient, since there is no mining. Stellar data analysis indicates that the transaction fee is equivalent to less than a cent for all analyzed transactions. Payment transactions (70.2%) dominate, in contrast to path payments (4.1%), in the analyzed records. It was observed that the majority of the payment transactions are micropayments (83%), whereas path payments transactions comprise of a more diverse mix of payment amounts. It can be concluded from the data analysis of Stellar transactions that the blockchain network is feasible for conducting micropayments. A comparative study of the characteristics as a micropayment system indicates that Stellar fares well in terms of providing micropayments. It provides support for regulatory compliance and AML/KYC procedures, preventing the usage of XLM in online fraud and dark markets. However, Stellar requires more focus on the non-technical characteristics of micropayment systems to expand it's user base and increase trust. The undertaken feasibility study of Stellar indicates that the blockchain platform is viable to function as a micropayment system and has significant potential to contribute to the digital economy.

References

1. Stellar Network Overview. https://www.stellar.org/developers/guides/get-started/. Last accessed 21 July 2019
2. Manasse, M.S.: The Millicent protocols for electronic commerce. In: First USENIX Workshop on Electronic Commerce (1995)

3. PayPal Inc. https://www.paypal.com/us/smarthelp/article/what-are-micropayments-faq664. Last accessed 5 July 2019
4. CNBC. https://www.cnbc.com/2019/01/30/facebook-earnings-q4-2018.html. Last accessed 20 July 2019
5. Business Insider. https://www.businessinsider.com/2019-media-layoffs-job-cuts-at-buzzfeed-huffpost-vice-details-2019-2?r=US&IR=T. Last accessed 15 July 2019
6. Poon, J., Dryja, T.: The Bitcoin Lightning Network: Scalable Off-Chain Instant Payments (2016)
7. Brainbot: Raiden Specification Document, Release 0.1 (2018)
8. Libra. https://libra.org/en-US/white-paper/. Last accessed 21 July 2019
9. Brave. https://brave.com/. Last accessed 2 July 2019
10. Coil. https://coil.com/about/. Last accessed 6 July 2019
11. Ramani, A.: Micropayments: A Viable Business Model. A project for CS 181, Stanford University (2011)
12. Gai, K., Wu, Y., Zhu, L., Xu, L., Zhang, Y.: Permissioned blockchain and edge computing empowered privacy-preserving smart grid networks. In: IEEE Internet of Things Journal (2019)
13. Gai, K., Wu, Y., Zhu, L., Qiu, M., Shen, M.: Privacy-preserving energy trading using consortium blockchain in smart grid. IEEE Trans. Ind. Inform. **15**(6), 3548–3558 (2019)
14. Lundqvist, T., Blanche, A., Andersson, H.R.H.: Thing-to-thing electricity micropayments using blockchain technology. In: 2017 Global Internet of Things Summit (GIoTS), Switzerland (2017)
15. Khan, N., Ouaich, R.: Feasibility analysis of blockchain for donation-based crowdfunding of ethical projects. In: Smart Technologies and Innovation for a Sustainable Future, Proceedings of the 1st AUE International Research Conference, Springer, UAE (2019)
16. Khan, N., Ahmad, T., State, R.: Blockchain-based micropayment systems: economic impact. In: Proceedings of the 23rd International Database Applications & Engineering Symposium, ACM, Greece (2019)
17. Accenture. https://www.accenture.com/us-en/insight-blockchain-id2020. Last accessed 1 July 2019
18. Ali, T., Clarke, D., McCorry, P.: The nuts and bolts of micropayments: a survey. In: CoRR (2017)
19. Pass, R., Shelat, A.: Micropayments for decentralized currencies. In: Proceedings of the 22nd ACM SIGSAC Conference on Computer and Communications Security, pp. 207–218. ACM, USA (2015)
20. Parhonyi, R., Nieuwenhuis, B., Pras, A.: The fall and rise of micropayment systems. Handbuch of E-Money. E-Payment & M-Payment, pp. 343–362. Springer, Germany (2006). https://doi.org/10.1007/3-7908-1652-3_25
21. Mazieres, D.: The Stellar Consensus Protocol: A Federated Model for Internet-level Consensus (2016)
22. Stellar/ go. Transactions that fail during consensus are ignored by Horizon. https://github.com/stellar/go/issues/309
23. Kniberg, H.: What Makes a Micropayment Solution Succeed. Institution for Applied Information Technology, KTH, Stockholm (2002)
24. Abrazhevich, D.: Classification and characteristics of electronic payment systems. In: Proceedings of the Second International Conference on Electronic Commerce and Web Technologies. Springer-Verlag, Berlin (2001)
25. Weber, R.: Chablis - Market Analysis of Digital Payment Systems. Technical University of Munich, München (1998)

26. Parhonyi, R., Nieuwenhuis, J.M.L., Pras, A.: Second generation micropayment systems: lessons learned. Challenges of Expanding Internet: E-Commerce, E-Business, and E-Government. IFIP International Federation for Information Processing, pp. 345–359. Springer, Boston (2005). https://doi.org/10.1007/0-387-29773-1_23
27. Khan, N., State, R.: Lightning network: a comparative review of transaction fees and data analysis. In: Prieto, J., Das, A.K., Ferretti, S., Pinto, António, Corchado, J.M. (eds.) BLOCKCHAIN 2019. AISC, vol. 1010, pp. 11–18. Springer, Cham (2020). https://doi.org/10.1007/978-3-030-23813-1_2
28. Stellar Lightning. https://www.stellar.org/blog/lightning-on-stellar-roadmap/. Last accessed 3 July 2019
29. GitHub Link for Stellar Data. https://github.com/nidakhanlu/micropayments-blockchain
30. European Commission, Cybercrime. https://ec.europa.eu/home-affairs/what-we-do/policies/organized-crime-and-human-trafficking/cybercrime_en
31. McGuire, M.: Understanding the growth of the cybercrime economy. In: RSA conference, USA (2018)
32. Compliance Protocol. https://www.stellar.org/developers/guides/compliance-protocol.html. Last accessed 7 July 2019

Community Cash: A Community-Based Cryptocurrency for Implementing Activity-Based Micro-Pricing

Kosuke Komiya$^{(\boxtimes)}$ and Tatsuo Nakajima

Department of Computer Science and Engineering,
Waseda University, Tokyo, Japan
{kosukekomiya, tatsuo}@dcl.cs.waseda.ac.jp

Abstract. In this paper, we propose a new local economic infrastructure —"community cash"—based on blockchain and activity-based micro-pricing technologies. Blockchain technology, introduced by Satoshi Nakamoto in *Bitcoin: A Peer-to-Peer Electronic Cash System* [1] in 2009, has had a serious impact on the virtual economy. It has realized peer-to-peer digital data transfer without the trust of third parties. On the other hand, activity-based micro-pricing alters user behavior through economic incentives. By combining these technologies, we develop a blockchain that runs on a new consensus algorithm, proof-of-contribution. This consensus algorithm alters the behaviors of the members in a community by distributing rewards for generating blocks as monetary incentives. We first introduce the system of "community cash," and then discuss future works that can be implemented in the proposed infrastructure as well as remaining problems to be solved.

Keywords: Blockchain · Economic infrastructure · Activity-based micro-pricing

1 Introduction

Offering economic incentives is a powerful way to alter human behavior. Similarly, activity-based micro-pricing [2] aims to influence human behavior by offering a small amount of economic incentives. However, it has been difficult to realize this idea because of two reasons. The first is that the human behaviors that can be detected using current technology is very limited. The second is the lack of an economic platform suitable for micropayments. This paper aims to provide a solution for the second reason using the blockchain technology.

Micropayments are difficult to realize because the cost of the transactions is often high compared with the price of the payment. In Lehdonvirta *et al.* [3], two approaches are introduced to circumvent this problem. The first approach is to bundle small purchases and form larger units. For example, many articles are bundled to form a newspaper and the newspapers for each day are bundled into subscriptions. The second approach is to deposit a certain amount of money in advance and make each payment using the money deposited. This model is implemented for public transportation using

© Springer Nature Switzerland AG 2019
M. Qiu (Ed.): SmartBlock 2019, LNCS 11911, pp. 66–75, 2019.
https://doi.org/10.1007/978-3-030-34083-4_7

smartcards, such as in Suica [4]. However, these approaches can only be used in limited services that people use frequently.

Therefore, we aim to build a new local economic infrastructure based on block-chain technology and issue an original cryptocurrency *community cash*. This study targets communities that have about 20–60 members, such as university laboratories or small companies.

Blockchain was first introduced in 2009 by Satoshi Nakamoto in *Bitcoin: A Peer-to-Peer Electronic Cash System* to realize peer-to-peer digital cash transfer. This has enabled peer-to-peer data transfer without the trust of third parties. Currently, more than 2,000 cryptocurrencies using blockchain technology exist [5]. Cryptocurrency is a *"medium of exchange, created and stored electronically in the blockchain, using encryption techniques to control the creation of monetary units and to verify the transfer of funds"* [6].

Community cash is a cryptocurrency issued on a new blockchain that uses an original consensus algorithm called *proof-of-contribution* (PoC). Consensus algorithms, in turn, are used to determine who generates the block and receives the reward. In PoC, the rewards for generating the blocks are distributed to the nodes depending on how much the node contributed to a community. Based on activity-based micro-pricing technology, we alter the behaviors of community members, motivating them to contribute to the community by offering economic incentives in the form of rewards from the blockchain. An increase in the contributions of each member will thus improve the community. In addition, the PoC algorithm can balance the contributions among members and avoid situations wherein contributions are concentrated on one or few members. The final goal of this study is to combine blockchain technology and activity-based micro-pricing to achieve a sustainable community whose members are motivated to contribute to the community.

The remaining paper is structured as follows. In Sect. 2, we review select literature on the subject. These works include consensus algorithms that work like PoC, Ubipay, and the details of activity-based micro-pricing. Section 3 details our approach and the system. We explain the components required for the system and the functioning of the PoC itself. In Sect. 4, we elaborate the analysis and future works. We discuss ideas that can be realized through an economic infrastructure in a local community as well as problems that may occur when the proposed economic infrastructure is deployed. Finally, we conclude the paper in Sect. 5.

2   Related Work

2.1   Consensus Algorithm

A consensus algorithm is a *"mechanism through which a blockchain network reaches consensus"* [7]. Since public blockchains do not rely on the trust of third parties, an algorithm to make an agreement if the transactions are valid is needed. Therefore, each blockchain uses a consensus algorithm. For example, Bitcoin uses proof-of-work (PoW) as a consensus algorithm, while NEM uses proof-of-importance. Each consensus algorithm has different characteristics, such as confirmation speed or fault tolerance rate. In this section, we introduce delegated-proof-of-stake (DPoS), which is partially similar to the PoC algorithm.

Delegated-Proof-of-Stake

DPoS is a consensus algorithm used in several blockchains such as EOS or LISK. It was invented by *Dan Larimer* in 2013, and originally used for BitShares [8].

DPoS is described as *"a liquid, representative democracy with token holder suffrage"* [9]. The token holders in the network vote to elect the block producers. The weights of the votes depend on the voter's stake (the number of tokens) and the block producers elected produces the blocks in turn. The elected producers have an incentive against malicious actions; otherwise, they risk losing all their votes and will be removed as block producers.

The number of block producers differs with the projects. For example, EoS has 21 block producers, while BitShare and Lisk have 101 [10]. Unlike PoW, by limiting the number of block producers, DPoS realizes a higher level of scalability. However, this approach sacrifices decentralization by limiting the number of block producers. Therefore, Konstantopoulos [10] recommends using DPoS for systems that require high throughput, but do not require perfect security—for example, using DPoS for the second layer for features that do not require high security; and using PoW for the base layer for the features that require high security.

2.2 Activity-Based Micro-Pricing

Activity-based micro-pricing was first introduced by Yamabe *et al.* [2]. It aims to alter human behavior by combining persuasive applications and electronic payment. Pervasive persuasive applications, in turn, are applications that aim to *"alter user behavior through the means of a feedback loop between sensor tracked user behavior and system output"* [2]. Free resources such as public toilets or plastic bags are often overused, in a phenomenon called the *tragedy of commons* [11]. To deal with these problems, it is customary to use economic incentives, such as charging for the use of plastic bags. However, these methods can only be used in limited locations. For example, customers can only be made to pay for plastic shopping bags at the cashier's point. However, activity-based micro-pricing combines persuasive applications to use this method in a wider range of situations.

Lehdonvirta *et al.* [12] find that a consumer's emotional response to the payment system also affects her or his behavior. Even if the amount of economic incentives is the same, the way it affects human behaviors differs based on how the incentives were given. Therefore, Yamabe *et al.* [2] consider four basic models with different incentive designs. The following two models are the models related to our study.

UbiPayment Model

Figure 1 shows the example case of the UbiPayment Model. When the consumer (shown as *customer* in the figure) takes a train, the consumer can choose either he/she takes the fully air-conditioned car or not. When the consumer chooses to take fully air-conditioned car, the system will charge the consumer small fee automatically.

In the UbiPayment model, consumers pay less initial cost, and then pay additional cost depending on their behavior. This model is based on Lehdonvirta *et al.*'s study [3], wherein, when payments are automated based on consumer behavior, the consumers showed reluctance due to the potential of incorrect payments. Since this approach tries to detect human behavior using mobile devices and wireless communication technologies, there is greater potential for incorrect payments.

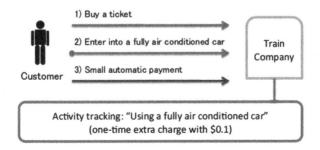

Fig. 1. Transaction flow in the UbiPayment model [2]

UbiRebate Model

Figure 2 shows the example case of the UbiRebate Model. When the consumer (shown as *customer* in the figure) takes a train, the consumer can choose what kind of car type the consumer takes, as in the example of the UbiPayment Model. The difference is, in this model the consumer receives small rebate from the system. However, the basic ticket fee will be higher than the fee in the UbiPayment Model.

In the UbiRebate model, consumers receive small amounts of money for their good behavior, which contrasts the UbiPayment model wherein consumers pay for bad behavior. This approach can eliminate the payment process in the automatic payment system as well as the possibility of incorrect payments that had made consumers reluctant in the UbiPayment model. This approach is also effective because people tend to buy items to receive points as rewards even though the item itself is more expensive [13]. Thus, the UbiRebate model can alter human behavior more than the UbiPayment model even if the amount of incentives is the same. In fact, the experiment in Yamabe *et al.* [2] reveals that the UbiPayment model is more effective than the UbiRebate model.

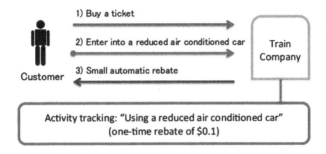

Fig. 2. Transaction flow in the UbiRebate model [2]

3 Our Approach

3.1 Overview

Figure 3 shows the overview of the community cash infrastructure. The infrastructure consists of three components, the blockchain, the community and the human detection system. In the infrastructure, the behavior detection system detects the contribution of the member in the community. When the contribution is detected the contribution score on the blockchain will be changed. Depending on the contribution score, the block-chain will distribute the rewards to the members in the community. In this paper, we discuss how the community cash blockchain runs with the Proof-of-Contribution algorithm and does not discuss about how the contributions of the member will be detected.

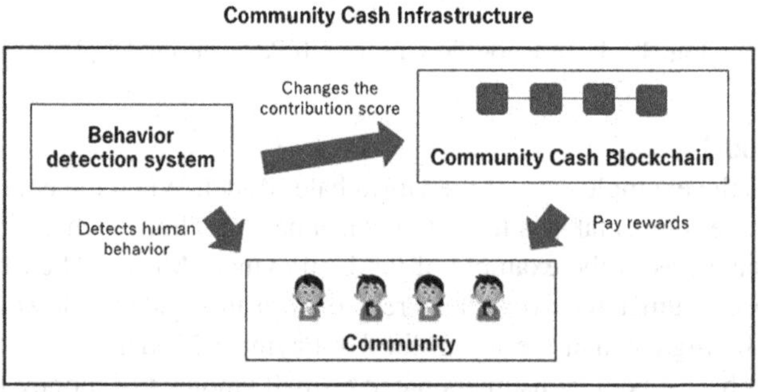

Community Cash Infrastructure

Fig. 3. The overview of the community cash infrastructure (Illustrations from *Irasutoya* [18])

3.2 Proof-of-Contribution

PoC is a new consensus algorithm used for the community cash blockchain. The algorithm is based on activity-based micro-pricing. In our approach, we alter the behaviors of community members by offering economic incentives using rewards from the blockchain. The rewards from the blockchain are distributed to the members in the node depending on their contributions to the community. As mentioned in Sect. 2.2, the experiment in Yamabe *et al.* [2] shows that the UbiRebate model works more efficiently in changing human behavior. Therefore, in our approach, the members in the community receive rewards for good behaviors instead of paying for bad behaviors.

3.3 System

Figure 4 demonstrates our *system*. The PoC design is derived from the DPoS (Sect. 2.1). The nodes vote for the block producers, namely, members who generate blocks and add it to the blockchain. While the votes in the DPoS are weighted by the voter's stakes, the votes in the PoC are weighted by the amount of the voter's contributions.

The block producers generate blocks to earn rewards and distribute part of the rewards received from the blockchain to voters depending on a voter's contributions. The order of generating the blocks is scheduled by the total weight of the votes the block producer has collected. When a certain block producer collects votes with more than 51% of the contributions, the block producer can undo some transactions.

The voters can change whom they vote for any time and must adjust accordingly so that a certain block producer does not receive 51% of the contributions.

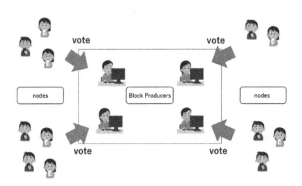

Fig. 4. The system of ***community cash*** (Illustrations from *Irasutoya* [18])

3.4 Rewards

When establishing a community cash infrastructure, initial fund N yen will be deposited and a new blockchain will be started, unique to the community.

The price of the community cash is determined by the initial fund N yen and the number of tokens M as follows:

1. When starting the blockchain, N yen is deposited for the blockchain and M tokens are issued.
2. $M/2$ tokens are distributed to the members in the community.
3. The other $M/2$ tokens and collected transaction fees are used for the rewards for generating the blocks. The rewards from the blockchain will be halved at a certain period just as the Bitcoin blockchain.
4. The price of the tokens is determined by the initial cost N yen and the numbers of tokens in the network (the tokens that are not burned).

Same as the Bitcoin blockchain, the amount of the reward will be the sum of the basic reward which declines as the blockchain becomes longer, and the transaction fee. However, to reduce the unfairness of decrease of the reward, when a member of the community leaves the community, the tokens he/she has will be burned so that the price of each token will increase.

3.5   Motivations

The motivations below are used to alter the behaviors of the members in the community:

1. *The motivation for earning economic incentives*
   The members in the community will receive economic incentives in the form of community cash tokens.
2. *The motivation for preventing malicious block generation*
   When the contributions to the community are unbalanced among the members, one or few members can monopolize 51% of the total contribution. If so, it would be possible to generate malicious blocks. To prevent this, all members would be motivated to contribute to the community.

3.6   Scenarios

Scenario 1: Earning a Reward from the Blockchain
The scenario of earning rewards from the blockchain is illustrated in Fig. 5. When the system detects behaviors that contribute to the community or cause trouble to the community, the contribution score is raised or lowered. When a block is generated by the block producers, the rewards are distributed to the members depending on their contribution score. The rewards thus increase the motivation of the members to contribute to the community.

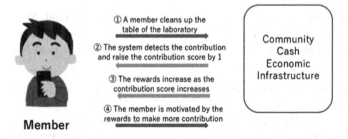

Fig. 5. Explanation of Scenario 1 (Illustrations from *Irasutoya* [18])

Scenario 2: Malicious Block Generations by the Concentration of Contributions
The scenario wherein malicious blocks are generated is illustrated in Fig. 6. When the contributions among the members are well balanced, the block producers cannot generate malicious blocks. However, when the contributions are concentrated to one or few members, they can concentrate their votes to a certain block producer. When the total weight of the votes exceeds 51%, the block producer will be able to generate malicious blocks. To avoid the generation of malicious blocks, members will be motivated to avoid the concentration of contributions.

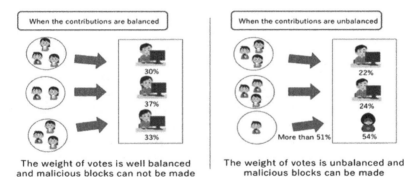

Fig. 6. Explanation of Scenario 2 (Illustrations from *Irasutoya* [18])

4 Analysis and Future Work

4.1 Remaining Problems

Detecting Human Activities

The difficultly of implementing activity-based micro-pricing lies in detecting human activities. Digital actions such as turning on and off digital devices are easy to detect, while non-digital actions such as reading comics or eating snacks are not [2]. Even though most individuals have their own smartphone devices, and hence some sensors or a global positioning system can be used, *detectable* actions are still limited. Systems like "Skynet" in China (天網) can probably be a solution. Skynet is *"the world's most advanced video surveillance system"* [14] installed in China, wherein more than 20 million artificial intelligence-equipped street cameras track and identify the ages and genders of pedestrians as well as the types and colors of vehicles. If these cameras can detect and identify human actions, it may be possible to actually implement activity-based micro-pricing. However, this idea involves a fatal privacy problem, making it practically unrealistic.

How Many Block Producers?

To maintain a distributed and stable blockchain network, the number of block producers should not be too small. However, block producers must have a device that is connected to the network and that can generate blocks the entire day. Therefore, it is difficult to have many block producers. If each smartphone device can act as a light node and add blocks by itself, it would remove the need to delegate to block producers.

4.2 Future Work

Nagesen

The Nagasen system can be implemented in the community cash economic infrastructure. The word "Nagesen" means "throwing money" in Japanese. In the traditional context, this term is used to mean giving coins to street performers for their performances. It is an example of a typical "Pay What You Want" (the person who pays decides how much to pay) economic activity, which is also used in services such as

YouTube Super Chat [15] or Twitch [16]. In these video distribution services, the audience watching the videos can pay money to the content creators if they like the video.

If the Nagesen system can be implemented in the community cash economic infrastructure, it would allow members to send a small amount of community cash tokens to other members to express positive feelings, such as "Thank you for cleaning up the table" or "The presentation was very good." In turn, the individual who receives the tokens will be motivated to also perform such actions. The main purpose of installing this system is to enable a lightweight process of expressing positive feelings and to enhance the intrinsic motivation of the community members.

Micro-crowdfunding

Micro-crowdfunding was introduced by Sakamoto and Nakajima [17] as a community-based crowdfunding infrastructure that motivates members to participate in society. Instead of using monetary rewards to encourage members to do tasks, this approach tries to increase the community's awareness by having members complete small tasks, such as emptying a shared garbage can. However, if this idea can be implemented in a running economic infrastructure, more realistic user studies can be conducted.

5   Conclusion

In this paper, we proposed a new local economic infrastructure based on blockchain technology. This infrastructure can be used to motivate members of the community to contribute to the community. To motivate the members, we proposed a PoC consensus algorithm based on activity-based micro-pricing. The members of the community will be motivated through two approaches: *economic incentives* and the *possibility of malicious block generations*. We also presented problems that persist despite our proposal and also described future works using the community cash economic infrastructure.

References

1. Nakamoto, S.: Bitcoin: A Peer-to-Peer Electronic Cash System (2009). https://bitcoin.org/bitcoin.pdf
2. Yamabe, T., Lehdonvirtay, V., Ito, H., Soma, H., Kimura, H., Nakajima, T.: Applying pervasive technologies to create economic incentives that alter consumer behavior. In: UbiComp 2009, Proceedings of the 11th International Conference on Ubiquitous Computing, pp. 175–184 (2009)
3. Lehdonvirta, V., Soma, H., Ito, H., Yamabe, T., Kimura, H., Nakajima, T.: UbiPay: minimizing transaction costs with smart mobile payments. In: Mobility 2009, Proceedings of the 6th International Conference on Mobile Technology, Application & Systems, Article no. 1 (2009)
4. JR East Suica. https://www.jreast.co.jp/suica/
5. CoinMarketCap. https://coinmarketcap.com/

6. What is Cryptocurrency: Everything You Must Need To Know! https://blockgeeks.com/guides/what-is-cryptocurrency/
7. What Is a Blockchain Consensus Algorithm? https://www.binance.vision/blockchain/what-is-a-blockchain-consensus-algorithm
8. BitShares. https://bitshares.org/
9. Delegated Proof of Stake: Features and Tradeoffs. https://multicoin.capital/2018/03/02/delegated-proof-stake-features-tradeoffs/
10. Konstantopoulos, G.: Understanding Blockchain Fundamentals, Part 3: Delegated Proof of Stake. https://medium.com/loom-network/understanding-blockchain-fundamentals-part-3-delegated-proof-of-stake-b385a6b92ef
11. Hardin, G.: The tragedy of the commons. Science 162(3859), 1243–1248 (1968)
12. Lehdonvirta, V., Soma, H., Ito, H., Kimura, H., Nakajima, T.: Ubipay: conducting everyday payments with minimum user involvement. In: CHI 2008 EA on Human Factors in Computing Systems, pp. 3537–3542. ACM (2008)
13. Mainwaring, S., March, W., Maurer, B.: From Meiwaku to Tokushita! lessons for digital money design from Japan. In: CHI 2008, Proceedings of the SIGCHI Conference on Human Factors in Computing Systems, pp. 21–24 (2008)
14. Big Brother is Watching You! China Installs 'The World's Most Advanced Video Surveillance System' with over 20 Million AI-Equipped Street Cameras. https://www.dailymail.co.uk/news/article-4918342/China-installs-20-million-AI-equipped-street-cameras.html
15. Purchase a Super Chat. https://support.google.com/youtube/answer/7277005?hl=en
16. Twitch. https://www.twitch.tv/
17. Sakamoto, M., Nakajima, T.: A Community-Based Crowdsourcing Service for Achieving a Sustainable Society through Micro-Level Crowdfunding, Internet, Politics, Policy 2014: Crowdsourcing for Politics and Policy
18. いらすとや. https://www.irasutoya.com/

Efficiency Issues and Solutions
in Blockchain: A Survey

Atabaev Odiljon[1,2] and Keke Gai[1(✉)]

[1] School of Computer Science and Technology,
Beijing Institute of Technology, Beijing, China
gaikeke@bit.edu.cn, odiljonatabaev@gmail.com
[2] Andijan Machine-Building Institute, Andijan 170100, Uzbekistan

Abstract. With the growing number of blockchain-based solutions in a few industries, we have moved to the next level of digital privacy. Meanwhile, several concerns related to transaction speed, data size, tracking information on public distributed ledgers faced to us. Time constraints and data overflow will lead to high financial expenses. In this paper, we address the efficiency issues of blockchain technology by reviewing recent significant work. First, we list the main challenges facing for efficiency. Then, we survey prior methods to handle efficiency issues studied by authors. Finally, we will discuss open challenges and conclude the work. This work can be helpful to determine future work directions.

Keywords: Blockchain · Efficiency · Consensus · Data overhead

1 Introduction

Privacy issues in data ownership are one of the main challenging fields of the digital era. Centralized systems have handled this problem for past years. However, it also has a few observable shortcomings as the centralized computing cannot guarantee a successful privacy-preserving for users when the third party is involved [1,2]. In many practical scenarios, middlemen are not considered a reliable involvement [3–6]. Personal data of users could be attached by some malicious parties or providers may use them for their own profit without asking permission from users. It certainly requires to use reliable, hard to tamper security methods to preserve user's personal data. As an alternative method for data protections, a time-stamping-based approach is deemed to be a potential reliable technical choice. A sufficient number of recent attempts have explored to discover adoptable solutions [7–9].

Haber et al. [10] investigated how to time-stamp a digital document in 1991. One of the methods to time-stamp the document problem, as they suggested, was called "distributed trust scheme". Most studies considered decentralization and distributed governance to be the main contribution of this work, until Bitcoin was introduced. Bitcoin has been widely believed as the first successful system created on the basis of Haber et al.'s [10] distributed trust scheme. Bitcoin is a

© Springer Nature Switzerland AG 2019
M. Qiu (Ed.): SmartBlock 2019, LNCS 11911, pp. 76–86, 2019.
https://doi.org/10.1007/978-3-030-34083-4_8

cryptocurrency system based on blockchain technology and it could change our thoughts about decentralized privacy [11]. Bitcoin blockchain uses distributed ledger technology to protect privacy, consensus methods to achieve fairness and blocks to keep data untampered with time-stamping. We know that secure and distributive nature of blockchain technology finding its place in finance, real estate, healthcare, human resources, smart trading, and other industries [12–15].

Currently, most applications of blockchain-based systems in finance and there are more than 2500 types of cryptocurrency systems on the network based on this distributed technology [available at https://www.investing.com/crypto/currencies/]. There have been significant work done related to privacy and governance of blockchain [16,17]. Lack of review studies addressed the efficiency of blockchain technology motivated us to discuss these substances.

In this paper, we mainly discuss recent achievements and some open issues challenging in the efficiency of blockchain technology. Even though many prior studies have focused on privacy issues and governance of blockchain-based systems, this work intends to concentrate on efficiency issues in blockchain. Different from other surveys, this work will discuss recent investigations and explorations on solving efficiency issues. There are at least two major reasons for investigating efficiency issues and solutions. On one hand, enhancing efficiency capacity is a primary requirement for establishing an adoptable blockchain system; on the other hand, the capability of preserving privacy highly rely on the operation efficiency while a real-time service is needed [18]. We will highlight open challenges that can be used as a reference for future research.

A few technical dimensions are covered in this paper, which includes the storage model, controlled block generation time, and consensus method of blockchain technology. Time constraints and resource intensities presented as the main shortages of blockchain technology [2]. This paper presents actual challenges and future work directions the on efficiency of blockchain technology. Main contributions of this work are given as follows:

- We focus on identifying the main issues that are challenging with the efficiency of the blockchain-based system.
- This work collects the experiment results from prior work and shows the efficiency of used methods.
- Deriving from the studied papers, we conclude open challenges and future research directions.

The rest of this paper is organized as follows: Sect. 2 gives information about existing problems and briefly define the questions of efficiency. Section 3 presents time constraints in the blockchain technology. Significant gaps in the resource intensity of blockchain technology given in Sect. 4. Section 5 describes Future Work and Discussions. Finally, Sect. 6 concludes the paper.

2   Leading Issues of Blockchain

Hereafter we address existing technological problems, and then we will consider recent proposed methods on improving the efficiency of blockchain-based systems in the next sections.

2.1   Time Constraints

While the blockchain came to solve double spending and Byzantine General's problems [19] it suffers from efficiency issues such as latency of consensus among nodes and transaction delays. As the consensus level is the base of blockchain technology, the latency of it consumes time, energy and requires high efforts. Achieving consensus by using less energy, time and lower effort is a key concept of the efficient blockchain system.

We observe that most existing blockchain-based applications suffer from latency due to the time cost caused by the implementation of consensus. Blockchain systems are designed to provide a decentralized and trustable environment without a third party. In decentralized systems transaction processing consumes a longer time than typical centralized systems and the decentralization setting is connected with consensus latency as well [3, 20–23]. Bitcoin system desired to achieve 7 transactions per second (TPS); Etherium achieved 20 TPS; Ripple could reach 1500 TPS [24]. However, compared to the existing centralized solutions, these efficiency capacities are far away from an adoptable standard. For example, VISA has achieved the maximum 24 000 TPS. Most current applications imply a challenge for blockchain-based cryptocurrencies as well as most blockchain systems being applied in the industry. Smart grid, telehealth, and other fields blockchain technology application needs to achieve faster consensus as it does today [3, 23].

2.2   Resource Intensity

Data duplication can be achieved due to the emergence of cloud systems, since the number of data copies is restricted by the amount of cloud datacenter. However, data duplication might be an issue in a blockchain application/system, as well as an issue from the perspective of efficiency. In the blockchain's distributed network, every single node should keep all transactions history in the local machine, which causes a potential data overhead in storage. Even though distributed ledger size of Bitcoin has reached more than 250 GB in the past 10 years, an efficient method of joining full nodes of Bitcoin community for lightweight devices due to the limited storage. Similar issues also apply in other blockchain-based systems.

Network bandwidth is another element from the perspective of resource intensity. For instance, a new joined full node of the Bitcoin community should download such amount of data to its mining machine. Typically, the download work is deemed a resource-harmful problem [3]. Many reports have suggested that being a full node in a mature public blockchain system require sufficient and strong network bandwidth supports.

Finally, energy supply also is an issue when consensus requires a higher-level computation. Different consensus protocols have been proposed until now. Every single method solving one main issue may recognize another, less addressed problem. Well-known Proof of Work (PoW) requires much computing power like nodes should have high-end devices to solve the cryptographic puzzle [25]. Besides, nodes will spend a huge amount of energy to attend in consensus as well as money and effort. Proof of Stack (PoS) which came to solve the energy-consuming problem of PoW. Nevertheless, it has another shortcoming, the node should have more assets to play in consensus with more benefit [26].

3   Solutions to Time Constraints

This section investigates a few recent attempts in the dimension of the time constraint.

A common research direction is improving throughput of the blockchain systems. Sakakibara et al. [27] have used In-Network Interface Card (in-NIC), Field Programmable Gate Array (FPGA) board to achieve a higher throughput. According to the study, the proposed approach is desired to achieve 100 000 TPS and the given experiment results suggest a proof. Besides, the latency of transaction confirmation equals to 7 μs. All experiments were done in 2 machines which is one of them assigned as a server, other is as a client respectively. However, implementation of such boards with more quantity of nodes have not been evaluated, which limits the quality of the evaluation.

Considering the advantage in data storage offered by off-chain system, Bai et al. [28] addressed the implementation of blockchain in industrial IoT. Due IoT devices have limited storage and bandwidth system should be light-weighted. BPIIoT utilizes on-chain and off-chain layers to apply it to the IoT devices. Sending-receiving transactions done in the on-chain layer of system while reducing bandwidth load and latency managed in the off-chain layer.

Our investigations also find that low throughput and consensus latency mostly are related to the mechanism of the consensus algorithms. Redundant phases in consensus may result in a longer block generation time. In order to increase the transaction speed and reduce block generation time, Xu et al. [23] proposed the group mining algorithm for PoW consensus protocol Multi Winner PoW (MWPoW). Moreover, Dlattice is a scalable permissionless blockchain system introduced by Zhou et al. [29]. The authors investigated the PANDA that combined DPoS and DAG-based consensus protocol. The PANDA consensus protocol is used when a fork in blockchain appears. The experiments suggest that PANDA achieve consensus among 500 virtual nodes in 10 s, which proves the scalability of the proposed method.

Some studies have tried to integrate blockchain technique with the existing security or trust management system. Wang et al. [30] studied the access control framework, which combined Etherium blockchain, interplanetary file-system

Table 1. Relative comparison of works on time constraints

Ref.	Method name	Technique	Function
[30]	ABB FDS	IPFS Storage, ABE security	High throughput
[27]	ABT SU FPGA-BNIC	NIC, Net FPGA, off-chain	100 000 tps
[32]	Fast SBS HASS	Fast BFT	Low latency, high throughput
[23]	MwPoW	Multi winner PoW consensus	Fast consensus
[31]	MChain	Two layer blockchain, background consensus, KP-ABE	Low latency, improved data storage
[29]	DLattice	Double-DAG, PANDA protocol	Scalable, low latency, 10 s of latency when forks appear
[28]	BPIIOT	On and off chain methods	Low load and delay

IPFS, and attribute-based encryption (ABE) technology. All data are saved in IPFS storage and blockchain is used to save the user's secret key. Implementing two-layer blockchain to improve security and latency of storage investigated by Bo et al. [31]. Liu et al. have proposed a [32] Fast Byzantine Fault Tolerance (FastBFT) consensus protocol. It utilizes combined trusted execution environments with lightweight secret sharing to achieve low latency and high throughput in network. According to authors considered consensus protocol can process 113 246 TPS in a network around 199 replicas (which are nodes). Table 1 presents a comparison for the reviewed work in the time constraint dimension.

4   Explorations on Resource Intensity

A resource intensity means that using a high amount/volume of resources to support blockchain-based systems. We surveyed papers addressed to storage overhead problems from dimensions of bandwidth, energy supply, and financial cost.

Dai et al. [33] addressed to storage overhead problem. They have proposed Network coded distributed storage (NC-DS) framework for blockchain. Framework puts the idea of distributing blocks among nodes instead of replicating them. Taking some number of original blocks from the ledger and with linear combination or shift and add way creates new blocks which are smaller the size and greater the number than original blocks. Then, these new blocks distributed to the nodes which all nodes have to receive on the new encoded block. Addressing the similar issue, authors of [34] work proposed Mobile Edge Computing (MEC) enabled framework for blockchain system which would decrease data storage requirements for mobile nodes. Meanwhile, mobile nodes could cache the computation task to nearby edge nodes. In order to avoid the load of nearby access points, nodes were able to offload the computational hard task to a group of nearby nodes. The study [35] had a distinct viewpoint on efficiency optimization, which used a novel smart contract to generate strategies of resource allocation.

Adjusting the block size is another thought for optimizing storage issue. Xin et al. [36] studied on the scalability of blockchain. By optimizing block size and construction they have achieved to reduce the required storage for private blockchain. Block construction optimized by selecting a special node to create the block. By giving a fixed number of minimum and maximum transactions that block can include. This influences to block generation time and as well as transaction verification time.

Table 2. Comparisons on resource intensity-related work

Ref.	Method name	Technique	Function
[36]	OADPB	Private blockchain	Optimized block construction, size, time control and transaction security
[33]	LSRRFDLB	NC-DS	Handles data overhead
[37]	MBDOE:REBBA	Avoiding futile transactions, express transactions, hollow blocks	Improves efficient using of storage, power and bandwidth
[38]	Proof of Personhood	PoP, PoPCoin	Fair decentralization
[34]	MEC EWBF	Mobile edge computing, computation offloading	Reduces energy consumption, cost and transmission for lightweight nodes, freeups storage in lightweight nodes
[25]	OmniLedger	Sharding, atomic commit, state blocks	High throughput, less latency, reduced storage requirement

Another study [37] work presented ways to reduce the storage use and effort by introducing a Futile Transaction Filter (FTF) algorithm and Proof of Collaboration (PoC) consensus protocols respectively. PoC consensus method presented on the basis of PoW and PoS consensus methods and takes collaboration credit (CC) as a stake and computation difficulty defined according to CC. Nodes will earn CC by producing blocks and from transactions included to the produced block. Just a few nodes will compete to create a block at the same time which may decrease significant waste of energy and effort as well. Designed FTF algorithm sorts transactions and keeps only important of them to further support blockchain-based system. If the transaction's output referred to the latter transactions this transaction will be omitted from the chain.

Proof of Personhood (PoP) consensus protocol has been proposed in literature [38]. PoP came with its cryptocurrency to named PoPcoin to prevent limitations of PoW and PoS consensuses. The physical and virtual parts of every node bonded together in order to create fair between nodes. Every node can use the physical and virtual machine to attend in the consensus process. In order to have an enhanced control capability on blockchain systems, a controllable consensus has been proposed in [39], which is designed to avoid the drawback caused by the pure decentralization.

The authors of the [25] work investigated the sharding technology to validate transactions in the blockchain system. The system called OmniLedger that utilized a higher-level available resources to achieve high-speed transaction validations. Atomix and ByzCoinX presented to carry out transactions faster via sharding and to increase DOS attack resistance respectively. Meanwhile, state blocks investigated to handle storage overhead which serves as stable checkpoints in PBFT. We present comparisons among resource intensity-related work in Table 2.

5 Future Work and Discussions

We provide some discussions based on investigations given in this work and discuss a few research directions for future work.

The efficiency of any technology is calculated by how less effort, materials, energy, money, and time spent to achieve the appropriate result. In general blockchain systems have distributed ledger to save the blocks and consensus method to create blocks. A problem of distributed ledger is related to spending materials, even if a single block has a small size (about 2 MB in Bitcoin system) as time goes by, and new blocks added to the system (every 10 min in Bitcoin, every minute in Etherium) ledger will have huge size. On the other hand, the system will spend energy, effort, money and time to achieve consensus among nodes of the distributed system to create blocks.

New nodes have to download blockchain data from neighboring nodes and also they have to download all transaction data from the IPFS network with the help of IPFS hash in blocks to check the reliability of data downloaded from other nodes. This is not a good moment when a new node must have big data-storage and a good connection to synchronization. The synchronization process needs further improvements. Besides this, the IPFS protocol itself is not production-ready-yet and its implementations are still in heavy development, which means blockchain network nodes may face with issues connected with IPFS protocol too. Our future work will address issues in the existing blockchain system and examine distinct technical routes to enhance the throughout performance.

The followings display two major research directions in our future work.

On one hand, we will investigate off-chain optimization mechanisms in blockchain. Cloud service offerings will be assessed to see whether and how off-chain solution can power up the existing blockchain systems. Due to the restriction of the block size, hardware-oriented cloud service is an alternative solution. The questions remain on a few aspects, such as how cloud-based hardware can be merged with blockchain networks, how cloud infrastructure offers consistent technical supports to blockchain infrastructure, or how cloud storage can fit in the requirement of the blockchain-purpose storage.

On the other hand, parallel computing-based optimization also will be one research direction in our future work. Networking structure will be explored to assess whether blockchain technology can be merged with graph theory [40–42]. A few challenges will be addressed in this field. First, the network structure is contradictive with the nature of current blockchain that relies on one single chain structure. Conducting a global consensus in a network structure is a challenging issue due to a few well known problems, e.g. double-pay problems. Second, network structure generally forms a bigger-sized network system, which increases the complexity of the workload so that, in most situations, throughout performance will be lowered down. Therefore, finding out an effective way to avoid the contradiction between the blockchain network size and efficiency performance will be a major research task in our future work.

6   Conclusions

Recently, interest in decentralized systems and network security has been manifested in the use of blockchain technology. The widespread use of blockchain technology in several areas, such as industry and finance, helps to solve some confidentiality problems and creates a more secure environment. Nevertheless, there are some problems with blockchain technology, which manifest themselves with new approaches. This paper considered efficiency issues of blockchain technology.

Acknowledgments. Authors would like to thank Ministry of Education of People's Republic of China and Ministry of Higher and Secondary Specialized Education of Republic of Uzbekistan. This work also is partially supported by National Natural Science Foundation of China grants (# 61972034), Guangxi Key Laboratory of Cryptography and Information Security (No. GCIS201803) and Beijing Institute of Technology Research Fund Program for Young Scholars (Dr. Keke Gai).

References

1. Guan, Z., Zhang, Y., Zhu, L., Wu, L., Yu, S.: EFFECT: an efficient flexible privacy-preserving data aggregation scheme with authentication in smart grid. Sci. China Inf. Sci. **62**(3), 32103 (2019)
2. Duan, Y., Sun, X., Che, H., Cao, C., Li, Z., Yang, X.: Modelling data, information and knowledge for security protection of hybrid IoT and edge resources. IEEE Access **PP**(99), 1 (2019)
3. Aitzhan, N., Svetinovic, D.: Security and privacy in decentralized energy trading through multi-signatures, blockchain and anonymous messaging streams. IEEE Trans. Dependable Secur. Comput. **15**(5), 840–852 (2016)

4. Gai, K., Qiu, M., Xiong, Z., Liu, M.: Privacy-preserving multi-channel communication in edge-of-things. Futur. Gener. Comput. Syst. **85**, 190–200 (2018)
5. Rizvi, S., Ryoo, J., Liu, Y., Zazworsky, D., Cappeta, A.: A centralized trust model approach for cloud computing. In: 2014 23rd Wireless and Optical Communication Conference, Newark, New Jersey, USA, pp. 1–6. IEEE (2014)
6. Song, Z., et al.: Processing optimization of typed resources with synchronized storage and computation adaptation in fog computing. Wirel. Commun. Mob. Comput. **2018**, 13 (2018)
7. Gai, K., Qiu, M., Zhao, H.: Privacy-preserving data encryption strategy for big data in mobile cloud computing. IEEE Trans. Big Data **PP**(99), 1 (2017)
8. Gai, K., Qiu, M., Sun, X.: A survey on FinTech. J. Netw. Comput. Appl. **103**, 262–273 (2018)
9. Gai, K., Qiu, M., Ming, Z., Zhao, H., Qiu, L.: Spoofing-jamming attack strategy using optimal power distributions in wireless smart grid networks. IEEE Trans. Smart Grid **8**(5), 2431–2439 (2017)
10. Haber, S., Stornetta, W.S.: How to time-stamp a digital document. In: Menezes, A.J., Vanstone, S.A. (eds.) CRYPTO 1990. LNCS, vol. 537, pp. 437–455. Springer, Heidelberg (1991). https://doi.org/10.1007/3-540-38424-3_32
11. Nakamoto, S.: Bitcoin: a peer-to-peer electronic cash system (2008)
12. Tschorsch, F., Scheuermann, B.: Bitcoin and beyond: a technical survey on decentralized digital currencies. IEEE Commun. Surv. Tutor. **18**(3), 2084–2123 (2016)
13. Kang, J., Yu, R., Huang, X., Maharjan, S., Zhang, Y., Hossain, E.: Enabling localized peer-to-peer electricity trading among plug-in hybrid electric vehicles using consortium blockchains. IEEE Trans. Ind. Inform. **13**(6), 3154–3164 (2017)
14. Zhang, J., Xue, N., Huang, X.: A secure system for pervasive social network-based healthcare. IEEE Access **4**, 9239–9250 (2016)
15. Liu, H., Zhang, Y., Yang, T.: Blockchain-enabled security in electric vehicles cloud and edge computing. IEEE Netw. **32**(3), 78–83 (2018)
16. Gai, K., Wu, Y., Zhu, L., Qiu, M., Shen, M.: Privacy-preserving energy trading using consortium blockchain in smart grid. IEEE Trans. Ind. Inform. **5**(16), 3548–3558 (2019)
17. Li, H., Gai, K., Fang, Z., Zhu, L., Xu, L., Jiang, P.: Blockchain-enabled data provenance in cloud datacenter reengineering. In: Proceedings of the 2019 ACM International Symposium on Blockchain and Secure Critical Infrastructure, pp. 47–55. ACM (2019)
18. Gai, K., Qiu, L., Chen, M., Zhao, H., Qiu, M.: SA-EAST: security-aware efficient data transmission for ITS in mobile heterogeneous cloud computing. ACM Trans. Embed. Comput. Syst. **16**(2), 60 (2017)
19. Fu, Y., Zhu, J.: Big production enterprise supply chain endogenous risk management based on blockchain. IEEE Access **7**, 15310–15319 (2019)
20. Uddin, M., Stranieri, A., Gondal, I., Balasubramanian, V.: Continuous patient monitoring with a patient centric agent: a block architecture. IEEE Access **6**, 32700–32726 (2018)
21. Liu, M., Yu, F., Teng, Y., Leung, V., Song, M.: Distributed resource allocation in blockchain-based video streaming systems with mobile edge computing. IEEE Trans. Wirel. Commun. **18**(1), 695–708 (2018)
22. Tsai, W., Bai, X., Yu, L.: Design issues in permissioned blockchains for trusted computing. In: 2017 IEEE Symposium on Service-Oriented System Engineering, San Francisco, USA, pp. 153–159. IEEE (2017)

23. Xu, Y., Huang, Y.: MWPoW-multi-winner proof of work consensus protocol: an immediate block-confirm solution and an incentive for common devices to join blockchain. In: 2018 IEEE International Conference on Parallel and Distributed Processing with Applications, Ubiquitous Computing and Communications, Big Data and Cloud Computing, Social Computing and Networking, Sustainable Computing and Communications, Melbourne, Australia, pp. 964–971. IEEE (2018)
24. http://cointelegraph.com/
25. Kokoris-Kogias, E., Jovanovic, P., Gasser, L., Gailly, N., Syta, E., Ford, B.: OmniLedger: a secure, scale-out, decentralized ledger via sharding. In: 2018 IEEE Symposium on Security and Privacy, San Francisco, CA, USA, pp. 583–598. IEEE (2018)
26. Zaman, M., Shen, T., Min, M.: Proof of sincerity: a new lightweight consensus approach for mobile blockchains. In: 2019 16th IEEE Annual Consumer Communications and Networking Conference, Las Vegas, NV, USA, pp. 1–4. IEEE (2019)
27. Sakakibara, Y., Tokusashi, Y., Morishima, S., Matsutani, H.: Accelerating blockchain transfer system using FPGA-based NIC. In: 2018 IEEE International Conference on Parallel and Distributed Processing with Applications, Ubiquitous Computing and Communications, Big Data and Cloud Computing, Social Computing and Networking, Sustainable Computing and Communications, Melbourne, Australia, pp. 171–178. IEEE (2018)
28. Bai, L., Hu, M., Liu, M., Wang, J.: BPIIoT: a light-weighted blockchain-based platform for industrial IoT. IEEE Access 7, 58381–58393 (2019)
29. Zhou, T., Li, X., Zhao, H.: DLattice: a permission-less blockchain based on DPoS-BA-DAG consensus for data tokenization. IEEE Access 7, 39273–39287 (2019)
30. Wang, S., Zhang, Y., Zhang, Y.: A blockchain-based framework for data sharing with fine-grained access control in decentralized storage systems. IEEE Access 6, 38437–38450 (2018)
31. Zhao, B., Fan, P., Ni, M.: Mchain: a blockchain-based VM measurements secure storage approach in IaaS cloud with enhanced integrity and controllability. IEEE Access 6, 43758–43769 (2018)
32. Liu, J., Li, W., Karame, G., Asokan, N.: Scalable byzantine consensus via hardware-assisted secret sharing. IEEE Trans. Comput. 68(1), 139–151 (2018)
33. Dai, M., Zhang, S., Wang, H., Jin, S.: A low storage room requirement framework for distributed ledger in blockchain. IEEE Access 6, 22970–22975 (2018)
34. Liu, M., Yu, F., Teng, Y., Leung, V., Song, M.: Computation offloading and content caching in wireless blockchain networks with mobile edge computing. IEEE Trans. Veh. Technol. 67(11), 11008–11021 (2018)
35. Gai, K., Wu, Y., Zhu, L., Xu, L., Zhang, Y.: Permissioned blockchain and edge computing empowered privacy-preserving smart grid networks. IEEE Internet Things J. PP(99), 1 (2019)
36. Xin, W., Zhang, T., Hu, C., Tang, C., Liu, C., Chen, Z.: On scaling and accelerating decentralized private blockchains. In: 2017 IEEE 3rd International Conference on Big Data Security on Cloud, IEEE International Conference on High Performance and Smart Computing, and IEEE International Conference on Intelligent Data and Security, Beijing, China, pp. 267–271. IEEE (2017)
37. Xu, C., et al.: Making big data open in edges: a resource-efficient blockchain-based approach. IEEE Trans. Parallel Distrib. Syst. 30(4), 870–882 (2018)
38. Borge, M., Kokoris-Kogias, E., Jovanovic, P., Gasser, L., Gailly, N., Ford, B.: Proof-of-personhood: redemocratizing permissionless cryptocurrencies. In: 2017 IEEE European Symposium on Security and Privacy Workshops, San Francisco, California, USA, pp. 23–26. IEEE (2017)

39. Zhu, L., Wu, Y., Gai, K., Choo, K.K.R.: Controllable and trustworthy blockchain-based cloud data management. Futur. Gener. Comput. Syst. **91**, 527–535 (2019)
40. Gai, K., Qiu, M., Zhao, H., Tao, L., Zong, Z.: Dynamic energy-aware cloudlet-based mobile cloud computing model for green computing. J. Netw. Comput. Appl. **59**, 46–54 (2016)
41. Gai, K., Qiu, M., Zhao, H.: Energy-aware task assignment for mobile cyber-enabled applications in heterogeneous cloud computing. J. Parallel Distrib. Comput. **111**, 126–135 (2018)
42. Gai, K., Choo, K.K.R., Qiu, M., Zhu, L.: Privacy-preserving content-oriented wireless communication in Internet-of-Things. IEEE Internet Things J. **5**(4), 3059–3067 (2018)

Technical Evaluation and Impact Analysis of Libra

Su-de Qing[1], Yi-hui Zhang[2(✉)], Hong-nan Liu[2], Tao He[2],
Bai-xue Yang[2], and Kai Wei[2]

[1] Key Laboratory of Mathematics, Informatics and Behavioral Semantics,
Ministry of Education, School of Mathematics and Systems Science,
Beihang University, Beijing 100191, China
[2] Cloud Computing and Big Data Research Institute, China Academy
of Information and Communications Technology, Beijing 100191, China
`zhangyihui@caict.ac.cn`

Abstract. Since the emergence of the concept of blockchain, it has always attracted the attention of the society and many enterprises. Some international giants have developed their own blockchain platforms to seize the market. Libra published by Facebook serves as a global simple borderless currency and financial infrastructure for billions of people. Viewed from the overall system, Libra is a blockchain platform oriented to finance, but its completion still needs to be improved. In this paper, we analyze the technical characteristics, verify its function and performance by actual technical test and evaluation results, and describe global impact of Libra.

Keywords: Libra · Technical core characteristics · Test and evaluation · Impact

1 Introduction

As an emerging technology, the decoupling and difficult tampering of blockchain has made it possible to reconstruct business models and create new industrial ecology in many fields [1]. From the perspective of its own technology development trend, the core technologies of blockchain such as distributed network, consensus mechanism, cross-chain, privacy protection, and system security are making breakthroughs in many ways to improve the overall technology maturity of the blockchain system [2–4]. Blockchain has several unique properties that can potentially address some of the problems of accessibility and trustworthiness. However, the existing blockchain systems have yet to reach mainstream adoption, and some projects have even aimed to disrupt the existing system and bypass regulation as opposed to innovating on compliance and regulatory fronts to improve the effectiveness of anti-money laundering [5].

On June 18, 2019, Facebook led the release of a white paper on the global digital cryptocurrency project named Libra. According to the white paper, Libra will serve as a global simple borderless currency and financial infrastructure for billions of people [5]. To achieve this goal, Libra has taken a series of measures. In terms of currency type, unlike Bitcoin, where prices are highly volatile, Libra will be a low-volatility

© Springer Nature Switzerland AG 2019
M. Qiu (Ed.): SmartBlock 2019, LNCS 11911, pp. 87–96, 2019.
https://doi.org/10.1007/978-3-030-34083-4_9

cryptocurrency supported by real asset reserves. In terms of core technologies, Libra is based on a permissioned chain that is open to the public to support smart contracts, and has improved key components. In terms of organizational structure, Libra is jointly led by Libra Association, which is a new technology-based approach to governance and decision making.

This paper focuses on which core technical characteristics have been designed and improved for Libra, and what are the evaluation and verification results from actual technical tests. Besides, this paper also discusses what impact does Libra have on the financial industry and the global economy.

The remainder of our paper is structured as follows: We present the analysis of libta core technical characteristics in Sect. 2. We lay out the technical tests and evaluation results in Sect. 3. We provide the libra impact discussion in Sect. 4. Finally, we conclude our paper in Sect. 5.

2 Analysis of Libra Core Technical Characteristics

The technical platform of Libra is based on a permissioned chain that supports open contracts to the public and is tailored to improve several key technical components for financial scenario objectives. Therefore, the Libra blockchain needs to achieve the following three goals in terms of the underlying technology (Table 1):

(1) High transaction throughput, low latency and efficient, high capacity storage systems.
(2) High security to ensure the security of funds and financial data.
(3) Flexibility to support ecosystem governance and financial services.

Specifically, for blockchain technology Libra has made significant improvements in two aspects: consensus protocol and smart contract programming languages.

Table 1. Comparison of Libra and other mainstream blockchains

Layer	Platform difference	Libra	Ethereum	Hyperledger Fabric
Application		Libra-coin Finance	Dapp/ETH	Enterprise Distributed ledger
Smart contract	Language	Move	Solidity/Serpent	Go/Java
	Sandbox	Move VM	EVM	Docker
Consensus		LibraBFT	PoW/PoS	PBFT/SBFT/Kafka
Ledger	Data structure	Merkle bucket tree	Merkle Patricia tree	Merkle bucket tree
	Data model	Based on ledger	Based on ledger	Based on ledger
	Block storage	rocksDB	LevelDB	LevelDB/CouchDB
Base component		TCP, P2P	TCP, P2P	HTTP2 P2P

Consensus Protocol: Libra uses a consensus algorithm based on a new Byzantine fault-tolerant algorithm [6], HotStuff. Compared with the traditional Byzantine algorithm, the HotStuff algorithm aims to support at least 100 verification nodes and can evolve over time to support 500-1,000 verification nodes with good scalability. To achieve this scalability, HotStuff differs from the traditional two-stage validation of the Byzantine algorithm, introducing a new phase that allows replicas to change decisions after voting without requiring a leader. This improvement reduces complexity while reducing the complexity of leader replacement. At the same time, HotStuff turned the traditional mesh communication network topology into a star communication network topology, which reduces the communication complexity of the system (Table 2).

Table 2. Comparison of consensus protocols

	Hotstuff	BFT	PoW
Member information	Need to know all participants	Need to know all participants	No need to know all participants
Performance	High	High	Low
Expansion	Expandable	Difficult	Expandable
Finality	Yes	Yes	No
Communication topology	Star	Mesh	Mesh

Smart Contract: In order to better implement custom transaction logic, a new programming language Move has been developed with security as the highest priority. Because the application scenarios of Libra focus on digital assets and finance, based on the First-class Resources philosophy, the Move language is designed to prevent assets from being cloned. Besides, the Move language fully draws on some experience of the Solidity language [7] in smart contract practices, so it limits or sacrifices a part of the flexibility of programming to pursue security. The Move language makes security isolation at a deeper level and does not support loop recursive dependencies, which could resolve the re-entrancy issue of smart contract (Table 3).

Table 3. Comparison between Move and Solidity

	Move	Solidity
Core feature	In the way of Resources, which can only be consumed, transferred, not copied or hidden	In the Value mode, which can be discarded or hidden
Flexibility	Low	High
Security isolation measure	Bytecode verifier Loop recursion not support	None
Secure	High	Low Relying on external audit

3 Technical Test and Evaluation Result

For verifying the function and performance of Libra, we have read and downloaded the program code from the Libra's official website, using 9 Kingsoft cloud compute servers for deployment and distribution[1] (Eight servers with eight-core CPU, 16 GB of memory, 300 GB of storage and 100 MBPS, another one server with 16-core CPU and 32 GB of memory). We have done the technical test based on the Trusted Blockchain Evaluation Specification [8, 9] and ITU-T FG DLT Baseline D3.3-Assessment criteria for DLT platforms [10]. According to the evaluation results, Libra basically meets the requirements of a blockchain platform. It was tested with 47 use cases, among which 22 items are required to be tested: 16 pass, and 6 fail. In 25 optional test: 7 pass, 18 fail. The actual test and evaluation results are summarized as follows (Table 4):

Table 4. Function test results

Part	Function test item	Pass items number	Fail items number	Not tested items number
1	Networking mode and communication	2	0	0
2	Data storage and transmission	2	2	2
3	Cryptographic module availability	2	0	0
4	Consensus function and fault tolerance	5	0	2
5	Smart contract	0	4	0
6	Deployment	1	0	0
7	Node management stability	0	4	0
8	System update	0	2	0
9	High performance solution	4	0	2
10	Parallel solution	0	2	0
11	Data volume control	0	3	0
12	Account and transaction	1	0	0
13	Account user classification and authorization system	1	3	0
14	Private key management	1	1	0
15	Signature and verification	2	0	0
16	Participants join and quit	0	3	0
17	Auditable platform behavior	1	0	0
18	Auditable user behavior	1	0	0
19	Auditable smart contract	0	1	0

The tests are based on the Trusted Blockchain Evaluation Specification and Standard lead by China Academy of Information and Communications Technology and ITU-T FG DLT Baseline D3.3-Assessment criteria for DLT platforms.

[1] This project is supported by National Key R&D Program of China (2017YFB1400704/ 2017YFB1400705).

(1) In terms of data storage structure, Libra iterates traditional "blocks" and it arranges and aggregates transactions through Merkle tree. In Libra consensus protocol, a certain number of transactions are packaged as "block" for batch processing, to optimize the consensus efficiency of transactions. But after making consensus, the "block" packages are still broken up into each transaction and use Merkle tree for data storage. In each transaction, the concept of version number is introduced, to obtain the latest status of the transaction by checking the latest version, to check the authenticity of the transaction by traversing the historical version, and to avoid a lot of computational costs of traditional blockchain when tracing to original block for verification.

(2) In terms of underlying database, RocksDB [11], which is independently developed by Facebook, has been chosen. Specifically, it is divided into two databases: consensus database for voting information and ledger database for historical information. Among them, the account address is anonymous without binding with the user's real identity. A user can create any number of accounts, which shows certain anti-regulatory characteristics.

(3) In terms of consensus protocol, the change relying on HotStuff brings efficiency improvement, but it does not consider dynamic increasing recruitment and other issues. The Libra consensus protocol inherits the characteristics of the Practical Byzantine Fault Tolerance (PBFT) and can only tolerate the spiteful behaviour with less than 1/3 nodes. By increasing the serial number, it can effectively prevent "double spending". Currently, Libra unites 27 international enterprises as partners. However, when new partners are added, the detailed process of dynamic addition and adaptation of consensus algorithm are not realized in its code.

(4) In terms of smart contract, it is advantageous to absorb the experience and lessons of Ethereum Solidity, but the smart contract language is not completely realized at present. Move provides a financial demand-only smart contract language with advantage which can be easily developed, avoid access to the underlying system and limit risky instructions. The disadvantage is the expense of flexibility. In order to achieve the design goal of security and controllability, large and complete smart contract functions have abandoned. From the perspective of code security audit, the original audited code with model design and controllable variables is extended to an achievable smart contract instance.

(5) In terms of open source, the maturity of projects needs to be further improved. According to the statistics online, after the project opened source, the community submitted a total of 87 error reports, of which 30 are still pending and 57 have been solved. The open source community is relatively active. The error reports mainly focus on that the current open source test now is just a basic implementation, without considering the complex environment of multiple operating systems, multiple terminals and multiple protocols.

(6) In terms of underlying network, Libra is only a basic network implementation, which does not consider the complex security problems of real production environment. Libra sends messages by using TCP/IP protocol and a message compression tool Protobuf to reduce the network loss on communication message. Libra makes public the client CLI user interface, but the remote invocation RPC has not disclosed. It does not use the TLS security agreement to protect security of communications, and does not consider firewalls between international enterprises. In this way, it needs to use the UDP protocol for network penetration and other functions.

(7) In terms of cryptographic algorithm, Libra adopts a universal cryptographic algorithm and does not adapt to the financial requirements of various countries. Currently, Libra adopts asymmetric-signature algorithm ED25519, which does not realize specific and localized cryptographic algorithms according to financial control rules of other countries. SM1-SM4 secret algorithm required by China's financial system is an example. In contrast, the hash algorithm adopts the currently most secure SHA-3 Keccak algorithm, which fully considers the situation where SHA-1 may be broken by Google and SHA-2 in danger [12].

(8) In terms of operation and maintenance, Libra has good system ease of use, but has many challenges in user management, private key security, access control and other aspects. On one hand, the system uses an account model, which has good readability, adaptability and operation friendliness, but has some disadvantages in complicating processing. On the other hand, Libra does not temporarily support hierarchical classification management for users, lacks secure and controllable private key management and retrieval mechanism, and does not provide multi-machine cluster distribution. It remains to be further observed how the whole system achieves efficient operation and maintenance.

(9) In terms of system performance, there is still a big gap between the current code and the design target. Libra has an average system throughput of 1,000 TPS, according to the white paper on Libra's website [3]. Therefore, the performance of the Libra platform, which bears the goal of global inclusive finance and cross-border payment, cannot meet the huge payment pressure of the retail market, and it needs to be combined with the centralized treatment. We have tested the Libra blockchain network with 4 nodes and 7 nodes respectively under a server with a 16-core CPU and 32 GB memory configuration, and conduct performance evaluation by sending multi-threading transactions from clients[2]. According to the performance test results, the transaction throughput of 4-node platform is 62 transactions per second, and that of 7-node platform is 45 transactions per second. Moreover, we have also measured the query performance of the system: the query performance of 4-node platform is 540 queries per second, and that of 7-node platform is 432 queries per second. Based on these index, Libra will encounter new challenges and problems when dealing with massive payments in the global market (Figs. 1, 2 and 3).

---

[2] Due to the current situation of lacking distributed cluster deployment for Libra source code, the supporting log tracking function cannot work in a distributed environment, so that performance data cannot be analyzed. Therefore, the final data is deployed in SOLO mode, with 4 nodes, 7 nodes and 10 nodes.

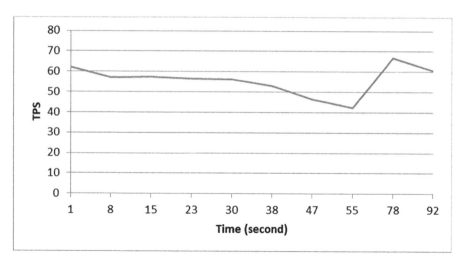

Fig. 1. Performance test result of 4 nodes

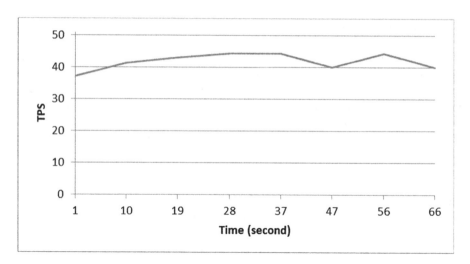

Fig. 2. Performance test result of 7 nodes

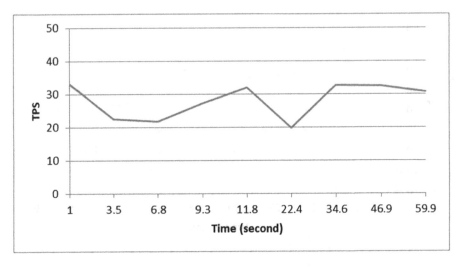

Fig. 3. Performance test result of 10 nodes

4   Libra Impact Discussion

First, the value of the cryptographic currency itself is inevitably influenced by the mortgaged credit currency. The cryptographic currency "Libra-coin" issued by Libra mainly use European and American legal currency assets as mortgage. Objectively, they will enlarge the country credit of European and American and rely on their political and economic security framework. Due to the various characteristics of blockchain technologies, Libra-coin will make global capital flow free and reduce global capital restrictions. Central banks may become more difficult to formulate monetary policy by strong capital constraints.

Secondly, Libra is not only a purely global currency, but also a global underlying financial infrastructure, which is supported by a underlying platform with smart contracts for global complex financial products, such as securities issuance, mortgage lending, etc. With more than 2.3 billion Facebook users and members of the Libra Association, the Libra ecosystem will increase the availability and participation of cryptographic assets, thereby expanding its reach and impact.

Thirdly, in traditional multinational organizations, many entities suffer high interaction and friction costs, making it difficult to achieve consensus and trust cooperation. The organization of Libra is a new model of deeply combining institution and technique. This model maps the rules of the real-world into blockchains by using code, which reduces the cost of trust, thereby enabling large-scale collaboration across countries and companies.

5   Conclusion

In this paper, we analyze the technical characteristics, verify its function and performance by actual technical test and evaluation results, and describe global impact of Libra. Viewed from the overall system, Libra is a blockchain platform oriented to finance, but its completion still needs to be improved. Currently, Libra's ledger design, data storage, consensus protocol and smart contract language MOVE, all reflect the technical characteristics and clear goals of financial system scenarios. However, from the perspectives of the integrity of the actual published code and the usability of the system, its completion still needs to be improved. The dynamic reinforcement of consensus protocol, the implementation of underlying network and encryption algorithm, etc., need to be updated by further iterations.

Acknowledgements. This paper's relevant project is supported by National Key R&D Program of China (2017YFB1400704/2017YFB1400705). In addition, this work is supported by Program of National Natural Science Foundation of China Grant No. 11871004, Fundamental Research of Civil Aircraft Grant No. MJ-F-2012-04.

References

1. Blockchain White Paper. Trusted Blockchain Initiatives. http://www.trustedblockchain.cn/schedule/detail/2990
2. Li, K., Li, H., Hou, H., Li, K., Chen, Y.: Proof of vote: a high-performance consensus protocol based on vote mechanism & consortium blockchain. In: 19th IEEE International Conference on High Performance Computing and Communications; 15th IEEE International Conference on Smart City; 3rd IEEE International Conference on Data Science and Systems, Bangkok, pp. 466–473. IEEE Press (2017)
3. Ma, C., Kong, X., Lan, Q., Zhou, Z.: The privacy protection mechanism of Hyperledger Fabric and its application in supply chain finance. Cybersecurity **2**, 5 (2019)
4. Dasgupta, D., Shrein, J.M., Gupta, K.D.: A survey of blockchain from security perspective. J. Bank. Financ. Technol. **3**, 1–17 (2019)
5. Libra White Paper. Libra Association Members. https://libra.org/en-US/white-paper/
6. Miguel, C., Barbara, L.: A correctness proof for a practical Byzantine-fault-tolerant replication algorithm. Technical Memo MIT/LCS/TM-590, MIT Laboratory for Computer Science (1999)
7. Lolisa: Formal syntax and semantics for a subset of the solidity programming language. http://arxiv.org/abs/1803.09885
8. Trusted Blockchain Evaluation Specification and Standard: Function Evaluation Method. Trusted Blockchain Initiatives. http://www.trustedblockchain.cn/schedule/detail/2993
9. Trusted Blockchain Evaluation Specification and Standard: Benchmark Performance Evaluation Method. Trusted Blockchain Initiatives. http://www.trustedblockchain.cn/schedule/detail/2994
10. Baseline D3.3-Assessment criteria for DLT platforms. https://www.itu.int

11. Yang, F., Dou, K., Chen, S., Hou, M., Kang, J., Cho, S.: Optimizing NoSQL DB on flash: a case study of RocksDB. In: 12th IEEE International Conference on Ubiquitous Intelligence and Computing and 12th IEEE International Conference on Autonomic and Trusted Computing and 15th IEEE International Conference on Scalable Computing and Communications and Its Associated Workshops (UIC-ATC-ScalCom), Beijing, pp. 1062–1069. IEEE Press (2015)
12. Mendel, F., Nad, T., Schläffer, M.: Finding SHA-2 characteristics: searching through a minefield of contradictions. In: Lee, D.H., Wang, X. (eds.) ASIACRYPT 2011. LNCS, vol. 7073, pp. 288–307. Springer, Heidelberg (2011). https://doi.org/10.1007/978-3-642-25385-0_16

Pharmaceutical Supply Chain Management System with Integration of IoT and Blockchain Technology

Jianfeng Shi[1]([⊠])(iD), Dian Yi[2](iD), and Jian Kuang[1]

[1] School of Software Engineering,
Beijing University of Posts and Telecommunications, Beijing, China
`shiningworld@foxmail.com`
[2] School of Information and Communication Engineering,
Beijing University of Posts and Telecommunications, Beijing, China

Abstract. In order to solve the problems of safety, trust, inefficiency and traceability of pharmaceutical products in pharmaceutical supply chain, a pharmaceutical supply chain management system based on IoT and blockchain has been designed and developed. To ensure the authenticity of data sources, IoT devices such as radio frequency identification (RFID), sensors, locators and QR codes are used to collect the current status of pharmaceutical products at anytime and anywhere. At the same time, with the help of the distributed ledger technology of blockchain, the system has realized the sharing and storage of data in each link of the supply chain, and ensures that the data are transparent, traceable and not tampered with. Finally, the permission control method based on the consortium blockchain was designed to meet the privacy and confidentiality requirements of some data. According to the results of functional tests, the system effectively improves the transparency of data in the supply chain, increases the safety of pharmaceutical products, and reduces manual operation, so members of the supply chain can benefit from a more open information.

Keywords: Pharmaceutical supply chain · Blockchain · IoT · Permission control · Traceability logistics

1 Introduction

The pharmaceutical supply chain is a functional network around the core enterprise. Through the control of logistics, information flow and capital flow, it starts from the supply of raw materials to the manufacture of intermediate products and final products, and finally sells the products to consumers [1]. A typical pharmaceutical supply chain is shown in Fig. 1. There are still many problems in the pharmaceutical supply chain:

(1) The lack of trust caused by information asymmetry

There are many types of upstream and downstream enterprises with large span in the pharmaceutical supply chain, and the information flow among members is not smooth and timely. On the one hand, the management cost of enterprises increases significantly; On the other hand, it is difficult for consumers to trace the source of pharmaceutical products [2].

© Springer Nature Switzerland AG 2019
M. Qiu (Ed.): SmartBlock 2019, LNCS 11911, pp. 97–108, 2019.
https://doi.org/10.1007/978-3-030-34083-4_10

(2) Counterfeit drugs

The lack of transparency in the production process and logistics process of pharmaceuticals tends to lead to unsafe and even counterfeit pharmaceutical products circulating in the market.

(3) Security problems caused by warehousing and logistics

Different pharmaceutical products have different storage and logistics requirements. For example, some liquid pharmaceutical products are required to be kept under a certain temperature, while others are required to avoid light [2].

(4) Low degree of automation

Currently, the pharmaceutical supply chain mainly adopts barcode identification technology. The same barcode code can only define one kind of products, and the scanner can only recognize one bar code at a time.

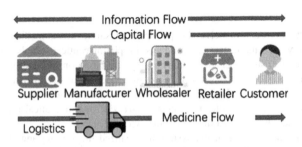

Fig. 1. Pharmaceutical supply chain

King uses RFID to secure the pharmaceutical supply chain [3]; Kumar uses block chain and QR code to achieve traceability of pharmaceutical products in the supply chain [4]; Aich analyzed the possibility of using a combination of blockchain and IoT in the pharmaceutical supply chain [5].

The above methods either fail to fully exploit the characteristics of the IoT and blockchain, or fail to take into account the special requirements of each member in the pharmaceutical supply chain between data opening and privacy protection.

To solve the above problems, this paper first uses various terminals of IoT to realize "comprehensive perception" of the production and logistics process of pharmaceutical products; Then uses the open source blockchain HyperLedger Fabric to build the consortium blockchain, and the distributed ledger technology realizes the "reliable storage" of data.; Finally, smart contract, symmetric encryption technology and asymmetric encryption technology are used to enable different members to have different data writing and access rights. While some of the information is fully disclosed, it also protects the privacy data from being acquired by other competitors in the same industry.

2 New Architecture Design of Pharmaceutical Supply Chain System

As shown in Fig. 2, the system is divided into six modules, which are the IoT module, the application module, the certificate authority, the transaction privacy module, the smart contract module and the Fabric blockchain platform.

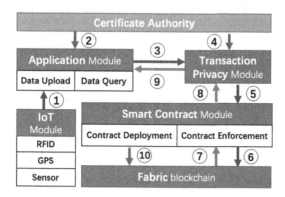

Fig. 2. Overall system architecture

(1) The IoT module is composed of many kinds of data acquisition devices such as RFID, GPS, sensors and their networks. As shown in step 1 of Fig. 2, The environmental status data of pharmaceutical products in transportation and storage is uploaded to the application module, as a reliable data source of the whole supply chain system.

(2) The application module consists of the data upload sub-module and the data query sub-module. As shown in step 2 of Fig. 2, First, the data upload submodule obtains the public and private keys of the current member institutions from the certificate authority. Then, as shown in step 3 of Fig. 2, the environmental data of medical products obtained from the IoT module, together with the relevant data of the current link node, are transferred to the transaction privacy module, and finally the client functions such as logistics monitoring are realized.

Users can call the contract program in the smart contract module to query data from the blockchain module through the data query sub-module, such as steps 7, 8 and 9, so as to realize the traceability of medical products and other functions.

(3) The certificate authority is responsible for generating the public key, private key, and version number for each member in the blockchain.

(4) The transaction privacy module is responsible for encrypting and decrypting the data uploaded by pharmaceutical manufacturers, logistics service providers, pharmaceutical commercial companies, hospitals, drug stores and other supply chain members, and sharing the encryption key among the strong relevant parties of the transaction, so as to ensure that the detailed information of the transaction of pharmaceutical products will not be obtained by non-relevant parties.

(5) The smart contract module is responsible for providing API to the application module, including the deployment, call, execution and logout of the contract. In step 5 of Fig. 2, When receiving the call request from the outside, each participating node distributes the execution of smart contract code, realizing the function of uploading data and querying data to the blockchain module.

(6) The Fabric blockchain platform mainly realizes the functions in three aspects. First, it connects the nodes of business participants through P2P networking. Every transaction needs to reach a consensus among different parties, and a new block will be generated after multiple transactions. The second is to store intelligent contract code as the basis of smart contract module call. The third is to store or return data in the blockchain, as shown in steps 6 and 7 of Fig. 2.

3 Comprehensively Perceive the Real-Time Environment State Based on IoT

3.1 The Application of RFID

RFID (Radio Frequency Identification) is a network system that uses the electromagnetic spectrum to transmit specific identification information in a non-contact, vision-free and highly reliable way [6]. With its large storage capacity, long-distance penetrability and batch reading, it can be applied to all kinds of environments and it has unique global ID number, which will completely change the traditional supply chain model.

As shown in Fig. 3, the RFID card reader sends signals at a specific frequency through the antenna. When an RFID tag enters the magnetic field, it picks up energy through an inductive current and sends data stored on the chip. RFID card reader receives the data and then transfers it to the application module for data verification and processing; Finally, the data is transferred to the blockchain module for storage through the network, so as to realize the data transmission and exchange of the whole system [7].

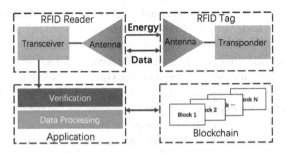

Fig. 3. RFID system interaction diagram

3.2 The Operational Process of the IoT in the Pharmaceutical Supply Chain

The IoT is a network that enables physical devices, vehicles, buildings and embedded electronics, software, sensors and so on to collect and exchange data [8].

Fig. 4. RFID Tags with QR code

(1) At the completion of pharmaceutical product production, each box of pharmaceutical products will be labeled with a radio frequency identification tag with a unique global code. As shown in Fig. 4, the information of the pharmaceutical product is printed on the tag surface by the RFID tag printer, and the information of the pharmaceutical product is written to the system by the RFID reader embedded in the tag printer, thus completing the information identification of the medical product in the RFID Internet of Things management system.

(2) The RFID tag selected here is fragile. After being pasted, if torn off, it will be broken, which effectively prevents the problem of fake products caused by repeated use of the tag.

(3) RFID readers are installed in transport vehicles and warehouses. When the pharmaceutical products with RFID tags arrive, the storage channel with RFID readers will automatically identify the RFID tags. According to the label information obtained, the warehousing operation of pharmaceutical products will be completed automatically, saving a lot of manpower and improving the accuracy of inventory.

(4) The system uses sensors to obtain the current geographic location, temperature, humidity, illumination and other information, and uses the unique code of the box as the index to upload and update the environmental status information of the box to the application module in real time.

(5) IoT technology can effectively realize the functions of positioning, tracking, monitoring and tracing in a series of supply chain links, such as production, distribution, transportation and warehousing of pharmaceutical products.

4 Break Data Islands Based on Fabric and Smart Contracts

4.1 Blockchain and HyperLedger Fabric

Blockchain is an integrated innovation based on game theory, cryptography and software engineering [9]. Its core lies in the trust relationship between each other established through distributed network, time-immutable cryptography and distributed consensus mechanism and other technologies.

Blockchain is an orderly chain data structure composed of blocks, as shown in Fig. 5. Each block in the chain contains the hash value of the previous block, which can be traced back to the first block (the founding block) by any block in the chain, so as to build an open, transparent, traceable and untampered value trust transfer chain.

Because the block header contains the hash value of the parent block, the hash value of the current block is affected by the parent block. Once a block changes, all subsequent blocks must be recalculated. When a block has enough subsequent blocks, any changes to it will consume a huge amount of computing power, so a blockchain long enough to ensure that its recorded information can not be changed, which is an

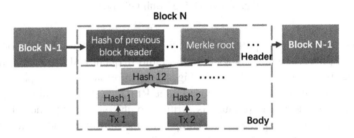

Fig. 5. Blockchain structure diagram

important basis for the security of the blockchain.

Hyperledger Fabric is one of consortium blockchain, which adopts the modular architecture, provide swappable and extensible components. It overcomes the shortcomings of public chain projects such as Bitcoin and Ethereum, such as low throughput, no privacy mechanism, inefficient consensus algorithm, etc. so Fabric is more suitable for business scenarios [10].

4.2   The Process of Building Transaction and Multi-node Consensus

As a consortium blockchain, Fabric logically decouples node roles into Endorser (endorsement node) and Committer (authentication node). The process of building the transaction is as follows [10]:

(1) The client obtains the identity certificate from the CA and adds it to the application channel in the network;
(2) Construct a TX Proposal and select the appropriate endorsement strategy to submit the transaction to the Endorser node for endorsement;
(3) Endorser node checks the validity of the transaction, executes the transaction, endorses the transaction result and returns it to the client;
(4) After collecting enough endorsement support, the client can construct a legitimate transaction request and send it to the Orderer node;

(5) The Orderer node globally sorts all legitimate transactions in the network and combines a batch of sorted transactions into a block structure;

(6) The Committer node periodically obtains the sorted block structure of batch transactions from the Orderer node, performs the final check on these transactions before listing, and then writes the results into the ledger after passing the check.

4.3 Smart Contract Module

Smart contract can be regarded as a program deployed in a blockchain that can run automatically. When the conditions set by the program are met, the smart contract will be triggered and automatically executed, realizing a series of functions such as data processing, value transfer and asset management [11]. Hyperledger Fabric's smart contract is also called Chaincode, and the smart modules of this system mainly include *manufacture()*, *wholesale()*, *ship()*, *retail()*, *trace_to_the_source()* and other methods.

Manufacture() is called by the pharmaceutical product manufacturer node and is responsible for writing the unique number, product information, manufacturer information, raw material supplier information, production date, batch information of each box of pharmaceutical products into the blockchain.

Wholesale() is called by the node of pharmaceutical wholesale company. The system obtains the unique number of each box of pharmaceutical products and writes the wholesale company information and purchase information into the blockchain.

Ship() is called by the node of the logistics and transportation company, and the system regularly writes the logistics node address, storage temperature, storage humidity, storage lighting and other information of the box of medicine to the blockchain.

Retail() is invoked by hospital and drug store nodes. After the box of drugs is purchased by consumers, the system obtains the unique number of each box of pharmaceutical products and writes the selling time, place, price and other information into the blockchain.

Trace_to_the_source() is called by the consumer node, consumers can scan the QR code on the pharmaceutical products packaging box through one smartphone to obtain all information of the box of pharmaceutical product.

Pseudo-code P.1: Smart contract framework for the medical supply chain

---

```
// Initialization Function
func Init(stub shim.ChaincodeStubInterface) peerResponse { }
// Invoke Function
func Invoke(stub shim.ChaincodeStubInterface) peer.Response {
function, args := stub.GetFunctionAndParameters() {
    switch function {
        case ' manufacture': result, err = manufacture(stub, args)
        case ' trace_to_the_source': result, err = trace_to_the_source(stub, args)
        // other smart contracts
    }}
}
// Main Function of Smart Contract
func main() {
    err := shim.Start(new(MedicalSupplyChain))
}
```

4.4   Transaction Privacy Module

Each member node may face the risk that the data will be acquired by other organizations or node owners, when uploading and storing data in the consortium blockchain. For example, manufacturer A and manufacturer B of the same type of pharmaceutical products naturally do not want their raw material supplier information, sales destination and other commercial information known to each other. So in order to solve the problem of data privacy on the chain, this system designs the transaction privacy module.

Firstly, symmetric key is used as session key to encrypt the transaction. Then the session key is encrypted with asymmetric key, Finally the encrypted key will be shared among members through the consortium blockchain.

In transportation and storage, the status information of each box of pharmaceutical products is encrypted with the corresponding key, ensuring that the data is only visible to the strong parties involved in the transaction. The specific process is as follows [10]:

(1) Pharmaceutical manufacturer A generates symmetric encryption key, which is encrypted by the public key (Pkey1, Pkey2, Pkey3, Pkey4) of pharmaceutical commercial companies, logistics companies, hospitals or drug stores with strong relationship, forming (Ckey1, Ckey2, Ckey3, Ckey4):

$$Ckey1 = Rsa(key, Pkey1) \tag{1}$$

$$Ckey2 = Rsa(key, Pkey2) \tag{2}$$

$$Ckey3 = Rsa(key, Pkey3) \tag{3}$$

$$Ckey4 = Rsa(key, Pkey4) \tag{4}$$

Rsa is a asymmetric encryption algorithm.

(2) Pharmaceutical manufacturers A encrypt the Original_product_data with key to generate encrypted pharmaceutical product information the Encrypted_product_data and send it to smart contract for processing:

$$Encrypted\_product\_data = Enc(Original\_product\_data, key) \tag{5}$$

Enc is a symmetric encryption algorithm.

(3) The encrypted <Cdata, Ckey1, Ckey2, Ckey3, Ckey4> is stored in the database;
(4) The logistics company requests and obtains the key Ckey2 from the smart contract, and then decrypts the key with its private key Prvt2 to obtain the symmetric key:

$$key = DRsa(Ckey1, Prvt2) \tag{6}$$

DRsa is the decryption method corresponding to asymmetric encryption algorithm.
  The specified data can be decrypted using the symmetric encryption key, such as:

$$Original\_product\_data = Dec(Encrypted\_product\_data, key) \tag{7}$$

Finally the logistics information TsData is encrypted with key and sent to the intelligent contract for storage, namely:

$$Encrypted\_Logistics\_data = Enc(Original\_Logistics\_data, key) \tag{8}$$

(5) Pharmaceutical commercial companies, hospitals or drug stores use the same way to encrypt and decrypt the status information of pharmaceutical products, and use key to encrypt the data to be uploaded, thus ensuring the privacy of the data.

5   Evaluation

5.1   Functional Testing

(1) Production: When a pharmaceutical product is produced, as shown in Fig. 3, a RFID tag with a unique global number containing the production information of the pharmaceutical product will be printed, then pasted onto the packaging box of the pharmaceutical product, and the production information will be uploaded to the blockchain.

(2) Logistic: Logistics company's transport vehicles and warehouses are equipped with RFID readers, sensors, GPS and so on. The RFID reader periodically or at important logistics nodes reads the unique number of the RFID tag of the medical products currently transported, and updates the current geographical location, temperature, humidity, light and other information to the block chain.

(3) Retail: After receiving pharmaceutical products, hospitals or drug stores can use RFID handheld reader to quickly count the batch of pharmaceutical products. They can also quickly check whether the batch of pharmaceutical products meet the requirements in logistics transportation. If not, they can choose to reject them to improve the safety of pharmaceutical products.

(4) Consumer: when consumers purchase the box of pharmaceutical products, as shown in Fig. 6, they can scan the QR code on the RFID tag with the mobile APP or manually input the unique number of the box of pharmaceutical products, as shown in Fig. 7, so as to obtain its production status and logistics status and judge its security. It is worth mentioning that after consumers purchase this box of pharmaceutical products, the information that the box of drugs with a unique number has been sold will be uploaded to the blockchain in the checkout process, so as to prevent the label and number from being forged and fundamentally prevent the occurrence of fake drugs.

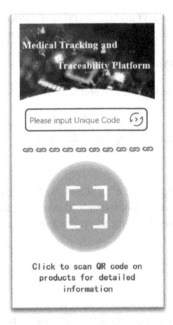

Fig. 6. APP - query interface

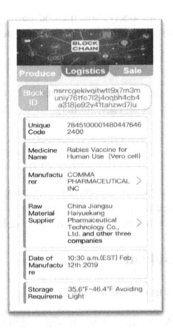

Fig. 7. APP - query results

5.2 Points for Improvement

(1) RFID reader can only recognize hundreds of tags at a time, if exceeded, there may be missed reading. At the same time, in the dense environment of RFID reader, co-channel interference will significantly reduce the reader's recognition performance, so the anti-collision algorithm of multi-tag recognition needs to be improved [12].
(2) Fabric only provides the permission control at the contract level, and cannot grant different permissions to different methods. At the same time, new algorithms need to be designed to implement the encryption of different secret keys for different parts of a group of data, so as to protect the privacy of different members more finely.

6 Conclusion

The pharmaceutical supply chain management system uses the IoT technology to realize the real-time state acquisition and automatic inventory of pharmaceutical products; Blockchain technology is used to achieve consensus among members and permanent storage of data, and a single node will not be able to modify the data; Symmetric encryption technology and asymmetric encryption technology are used to solve the confidentiality problem of private data between members. The system breaks down data silos between companies, increases information transparency, automates processes, improves security and even prevents counterfeit drugs from circulating on the market.

References

1. Yang, C., Zheng, Z.: Analysis on pharmaceutical supply chain in china and its operational process. Logist. Sci-Tech **34**(3), 54–56 (2011)
2. Liang, L.: Analysis of supply chain finance development based on block chain technology: a case study of pharmaceutical industry. Chin. J. Commer. **25**, 7–8 (2018)
3. King, B., Zhang, X.: Securing the pharmaceutical supply chain using RFID. In: International Conference on Multimedia and Ubiquitous Engineering. IEEE (2007)
4. Kumar, R., Tripathi, R.: Traceability of counterfeit medicine supply chain through Blockchain. In: 2019 11th International Conference on Communication Systems and Networks (COMSNETS), Bengaluru, India, pp. 568–570 (2019). https://doi.org/10.1109/comsnets.2019.8711418
5. Aich, S., Chakraborty, S., Sain, M., Lee, H., Kim, H.: A review on benefits of IoT integrated Blockchain based supply chain management implementations across different sectors with case study. In: 2019 21st International Conference on Advanced Communication Technology (ICACT), PyeongChang Kwangwoon_Do, Korea (South), pp. 138–141 (2019). https://doi.org/10.23919/icact.2019.8701910
6. Yu, W., Huang, S.: Traceability of food safety based on block chain and RFID technology. 2018 11th International Symposium on Computational Intelligence and Design (ISCID), Hangzhou, China, pp. 339–342 (2018). https://doi.org/10.1109/iscid.2018.00083

7. Mo, B., Su, K., Wei, S., Liu C., Guo, J.: A solution for Internet of Things based on Blockchain technology. In: 2018 IEEE International Conference on Service Operations and Logistics, and Informatics (SOLI), Singapore, pp. 112–117 (2018). https://doi.org/10.1109/soli.2018.8476777

8. Yang, Y., Mao, J., Hu, C.: Study on the application of safe RFID and block chain technology in the anti counterfeiting and traceability of bottled wine. Appl. IC **35**(3), 66–69 (2018)

9. Chen, S., Shi, R., Ren, Z., Yan, J., Shi Y., Zhang, J.: A Blockchain-based supply chain quality management framework. 2017 IEEE 14th International Conference on e-Business Engineering (ICEBE), Shanghai, pp. 172–176 (2017). https://doi.org/10.1109/icebe.2017.34

10. Zhu, T., Yao, X., Xu, Y., et al: Cross-border remittance tracing platform based on fabric. J. Cyber Secur. **3**(3) (2018)

11. Arumugam, S., et al.: IOT enabled smart logistics using smart contracts. In: 2018 8th International Conference on Logistics, Informatics and Service Sciences (LISS), Toronto, ON, pp. 1–6 (2018). https://doi.org/10.1109/liss.2018.8593220

12. Wang, Y., She, K., et al.: Research on identification performance of RFID systems in circumstance of dense readers. Mod. Electron. Tech. **9**, 43–46 (2014)

Securing Intelligent Transportation System: A Blockchain-Based Approach with Attack Mitigation

Le Su[1,2(✉)], Yao Cheng[2], Huasong Meng[2,3], Vrizlynn Thing[2,3], Zhe Wang[4], Linghe Kong[4], and Long Cheng[5]

[1] Nanyang Technological University, Singapore, Singapore
le.su@ntu.edu.sg
[2] Institute for Infocomm Research, Singapore, Singapore
[3] National University of Singapore, Singapore, Singapore
[4] Shanghai Jiao Tong University, Shanghai, China
[5] Clemson University, Clemson, USA

Abstract. In recent years, the intelligent transportation system has become an inseparable component for the smart city ecosystem. Through information sharing among the entities in the ITS such as roadside units, traffic cameras and local controllers, the entire system aims at improving road safety and overall traffic efficiency. However, as drastic amount of data have been exchanged and logged, how could such a system maintain the integrity, authenticity, and non-repudiation of the information for constant verification and audit is one of the biggest challenges. At the same time, as being considered as part of the critical infrastructure, in the smart city ecosystem, the security of the ITS also needs to be addressed carefully. In this work, we propose a novel blockchain-based architecture for ITS, to record actions and information sharing among the entities, at the same time assist in mitigating common types of attacks. Experiments are conducted to assess the overhead of critical cryptographic primitives.

Keywords: Blockchain · Intelligent transport · Data recording · Security · Attack mitigation

1 Introduction

The Intelligent Transportation System (ITS) has become an inseparable component for the smart city ecosystem. The modern data-driven ITS [1] functions based on rich data collected from multiple sources such as connected vehicles, inductive-loop detectors, sensors, and traffic cameras. Accordingly, ITS runs various algorithms based on these data such as optimal traffic light decision and statistical traffic data analysis. Compared to the traditional transportation system whose objective is to facilitate the orderly traffic flow, the modern data-driven ITS aims at both orderly and timely traffic flow by optimizing the use of the existing transportation infrastructure, enhancing overall traffic efficiency,

© Springer Nature Switzerland AG 2019
M. Qiu (Ed.): SmartBlock 2019, LNCS 11911, pp. 109–119, 2019.
https://doi.org/10.1007/978-3-030-34083-4_11

and improving road safety. As an infrastructure that is closely related to personal safety, the corresponding security, reliability, and stability of an ITS are the prerequisite for all the benefits it brings.

Technically, ITS is a highly distributed system with heterogeneous subsystems in terms of both hardware and software. There is a centralized ITS center for the purpose of overview, management and policy adjustment based on the data from the subsystems under its regime. Under the regime of the ITS center, there are thousands of local controllers deployed out in the field. Local controllers strive to derive actionable intelligence from connected smart devices and sensors. According to the rich information it gathers, the local controller is able to make timely distributed decisions that fulfill the overall aim of the ITS system.

Despite the common threats to an information communication system, ITS faces several severe challenges caused by its distributed and heterogeneous nature. Firstly, ITS is a target with multiple attack vectors. The attacker can choose to compromise the sensors or the local controller to achieve her goal. For example, to cause slow traffic or a bad jam, the attacker can force ITS to come to an incorrect decision by impersonating the sensor, falsifying the data, or tampering with the decision-making algorithm. Secondly, the large number of heterogeneous sensors in ITS poses a great challenge in guaranteeing the data authenticity, which is essential to ITS since the authentic data is the foundation for an optimal decision. For different sensors with various specifications, it requires a specific effort to make sure the provided data is authentic. Thirdly, in case any attack happens, the distributed nature of ITS makes it difficult to carry out an efficient post-security audit. It is a cumbersome task to inspect a large number of distributed devices. In addition, the distributed storages may not be reliable since they are facing the threat of being tampered with.

With the above challenges in mind, we propose *SecBITS*, a *Secured Blockchain-based ITS*. The blockchain intrinsically fits the scenario in the ITS system where the algorithms are executed on the data from the decentralized smart devices and sensors. Briefly, SecBITS is able to record the sensor data and the decisions based on that data in a tamper-proof blockchain. Every sensor data and the corresponding decision are associated with a piece of smart contract, so that the data authenticity and the decision correctness are guaranteed. We also introduce specific contract terms to counter against certain attacks. Our contributions are:

- Propose a novel architecture for ITS based on blockchain called SecBITS which could enhance the ITS security by mitigating certain types of attacks.
- Provide security analysis on the capability of SecBITS in mitigating record tampering, DoS attack, rogue sensor attack, and logic compromising.
- Further carry out experiments to assess the overhead of critical infrastructure primitives such as cryptographic computations.

2   Related Work

Intelligent transport system (ITS) is the modern transportation system that applies information and communication technologies to infrastructures and vehicles to achieve efficient and effective traffic and mobility management. ITS is also referred to as data-driven ITS since it heavily relies on data from sensors (e.g., cameras [2], laser radars [3]) and vehicles [4] to estimate a real-time road condition based on which optimal traffic-related decisions such dynamic traffic light signal timings are made. In terms of data flow in ITS, vehicles report data through DSRC (Dedicated Short Range Communications) to the RSU (Roadside Unit) [5]. RSUs, as well as various sensors feed their collected data to the local controller, which is a microcomputer located near the intersection. The local controller is responsible for making real-time local traffic light decisions based on the fed data and issuing traffic light command. Such ITS architecture is common in nowadays and more details about it can be found in related literature [1]. Despite the architecture and technique have been widely studied, the security of ITS has rarely been analyzed. The goal of our work is to propose a secured ITS design with the help of the novel blockchain techniques.

Recently, there is a stream of research on the blockchain application to CPS scenarios. Boudguiga et al. [6] analyzed how the use of blockchain can meet the requirements of confidentiality, integrity and availability during the Internet of Things (IoT) updates. In [7] the authors provided a high-level description of the adaptation of blockchain into ITS and furnished a particular case study on ride-sharing. However technical details on how to achieve such a blockchain-based system are lacking and no experiment testing on feasibility have been provided. The authors of [8] discussed vehicular ad-hoc network based on blockchain, similarly, only a high-level description over the concept was provided. Another work [9] studied the problem of using blockchain for simplifying the distributed key management in a heterogeneous vehicular communication system, whereby the communication and computation overhead could be reduced due to the blockchain system employed. Besides, there are also works focusing on the blockchain-based vehicular network in smart city [10] and inter-vehicle data sharing [11]. However, none of the above literature has conducted a systematic analysis of the defense capability of their proposed architecture against specific attacks so far.

3   System Design

3.1   System Overview

A typical ITS could usually be segregated into three layers. At the bottom are those data collection devices (or basic infrastructure) such as sensors, RSUs, cameras, etc. They constantly collect traffic information and send to the second layer, the local controllers (LC). With the traffic data obtained from nearby devices and possibly other information from adjacent LCs, the LC at a particular intersection then makes the decision for the traffic light timing adjustment. All these data and action taken could be sent to the top ITS center (ITSC) layer for storage, further processing, analysis, and traffic optimization. The entire ITS naturally forms a distributed network, where each entity is capable of communicating to others for information exchange. This property lays the foundation for empowering a blockchain framework on top of the current ITS.

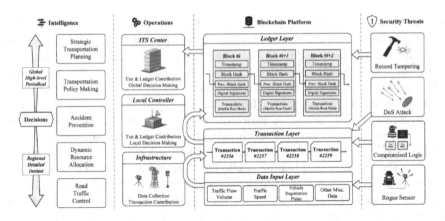

Fig. 1. SecBITS architecture

SecBITS is built upon a *permissioned* blockchain system. In such a permissioned system, access control is enforced and one could only act based on the rights granted to her. We define three types of access rights in SecBITS:

Read: allows the system participant to view the historical record of the system

Write: refers to the capability of submitting a "transaction" into the system, of which contains traffic information (either data or action).

Verify: allows the system designated entities to validate the transactions written by other participants, and form them into immutable blocks. This action is similar to the commonly understood "mining" process in the Bitcoin system.

To assign the access rights to the entities in different system layers, we consider their typical roles in an ITS, and their storage and computational capability. The data collection devices at the bottom layer will have the *read* and *write* capability only, as they are usually resource-constrained. Further, as typically the security protection over these devices are limited, granting them *verify* capability may affect the overall system security. The middle layer LCs and the upper layer ITSC will have the full access rights, particularly the ITSC might comprise a set of designated servers within its premise. The ITSC, as the authority, grants the different rights to the entities.

Each entity in SecBITS could be uniquely identified by its public key, generated and issued by the ITSC. Associated with the public key, a private digital signature signing key is also provided and should be stored locally at each entity. We assume the LCs and the servers under the control of ITSC have reasonable storage and computational capacity to perform operations such as digital signature generation, verification, and hash computation. The devices at the bottom layer only have basic functionalities, such as storing its own private key, a list of public keys and perform signature generation when data need to be transmitted.

Figure 1 provides a system overview for the proposed SecBITS. The overall system is segregated into four different pillars. The "Intelligence" pillar provides a list of exemplary actions in an ITS, sorted based on the characteristics such as time-relevance and geographical impact. "Operations" maps and reflects the three layers of ITS discussed above: the infrastructure for data collection, local controller for regional traffic decision making and ITS center as the governing entity. The "Blockchain Platform" is segregated into three layers as well, where the raw traffic data are submitted to the system and forms the transaction layer. The system designated entities such as LCs will verify the transactions and form the ledgers. The rightmost pillar, "Security Threats" lists four attacks that may occur at different layers and will be discussed further in a later section.

3.2   Transaction, Smart Contract, Block and Consensus

Transaction. One of the fundamental differences between SecBITS and the Bitcoin blockchain system is the definition of *transaction*. Instead of the traditional intuition of reflecting a financial exchange, in SecBITS the term refers to a broader and more generic concept: a transaction is a recorded activity between two parties, of which may contain data exchange or decision executed. We define three types of transactions. All actions could be covered by one of them.

Entity registration: the system requires each participating entity to register itself and record this action. The parties involved in this transaction would be the registering entity, and the ITSC. Information to be recorded could include entity public key, device type, geographic location, access rights, etc.

Data transmission: the data transmission transaction is to record the data exchange between two parties, typically from the lower layer devices to the LCs, and from LCs to the ITSC. This type of transaction will trigger the smart contract to make traffic light decisions.

Decision transmission: when a decision has been made, the corresponding decision-making entity will generate a transaction to send the instruction for execution. Although one could consider the decision transmitted is also a type of data, we separate this from the above for ease of exposition.

Figure 2 illustrates the format of a transaction. It contains three main fields, the transaction header, payload, and digital signature. The header includes basic information such as the IDs, the timestamp and transaction type, where the payload will include the data or decision to be conveyed between the parties. The digital signature field is included to assure the integrity and authenticity of this particular transaction. The signature is generated by the transaction sender and is based on the transaction header and payload.

Smart Contract. In SecBITS, the logic for controlling the traffic condition is embedded into a smart contract, where different smart contracts could be implemented for each intersection based on its location, past traffic data, etc. These contracts are further stored in a duplicated and decentralized way within each capable nodes such as LCs. As each smart contract has its unique identifier, it could be considered as part of the system entity, that is, same as the devices and LCs, but just virtual instead of physical. One would be able to communicate with the smart contract directly by sending a transaction including the smart contract identifier as the receiver ID, and structure the payload accordingly.

Block. Transactions generated by the entities will be broadcast into the entire network for verification, before they could be immutably recorded into the ledger, in the form of "blocks". Figure 3 illustrates the key components included in a block.

Transaction Header	transaction type
	sender ID
	receiver ID
	timestamp
Payload	traffic data, decision, ...
Digital Signature	digital signature by sender

Fig. 2. Transaction format

Block Identifier	Hash of current block
Block Header	Timestamp
	Miner ID
	Previous block's identifier
	Proof of consensus
Payload	List of enclosed transactions
Digital Signature	Digital signature signed by the miner

Fig. 3. Block format

Each block contains a block identifier, a header, the payload, and the digital signature field. The block identifier is the hash output of the concatenation of the header and payload fields. This identifier will be used for the next block generation in the aim of chaining the blocks together. The header field contains information such as timestamp, miner ID (the identifier of the entity who creates this block), the previous block identifier (as to chain the blocks), and proof of consensus. The payload includes all the transactions details collected by the miner for the past epoch. The digital signature is created based on the concatenation of the first three fields.

Consensus Protocol. In SecBITS, we employ Byzantine Fault Tolerance (BFT) protocol. For each time period where a block needs to be formed, according to the protocol, the SecBITS will select one "leader" from the designated entities (e.g., the LCs and servers under ITSC's control). This leader will collect the unconfirmed transactions, form a block as illustrated above and include its ID into the miner ID field. This particular block will be broadcast to the entire network and verified by the community. As long as the number of successful verification passes a threshold, this particular block is considered as valid and written into the ledger. The "proof-of-consensus" to be included are the digital signatures generated by the entities who have successfully verified the blocks.

BFT is a well-studied protocol with many variants. By selecting different variants, the algorithm execution procedure could slightly differ and the consensus threshold level could be adjusted based on the security level required. For the basic BFT scheme where the threshold is set to be 2/3, an attacker still needs to compromise at least 1/3 of the entities to launch a successful attack, which is almost impossible considering the number of entities in the system.

4 Security Analysis

In this section, we discuss four different types of attacks that the SecBITS could assist in prevention and thus enhancing the security of the entire ITS.

Record Tampering. The ITS continuously collects, processes and records a large amount of data such as road condition reported from RSUs and local controllers, as well as log information that include decisions made based on the reported data. This information are stored at either LCs or ITSC with different granularity and lifetime, for later analysis, decision making, and investigation. Although different approaches could be enforced, such as enhancing the firewall for protecting the data storage server, or using digital signatures for each data block to ensure integrity, this recorded information are still subjected to tampering, as firewalls could be breached and signing keys could be compromised.

The proposed SecBITS provides additional assurance for record security due to the data block chaining nature of the blockchain itself. That collected information are validated, "mined" and chained together by the system designated entities to form immutable data blocks. Assume at the time of the attack, there exist n many blocks. An attacker (regardless of insider or outsider) who attempts to manipulate a particular transaction which is contained in block b_k from the current chain would need to re-generate all the block hashing from block b_k to b_n based on the block contents. Further, all the signatures that are contained in the affected blocks need to be re-computed based on the new block hash. This is almost impractical as the attacker needs to breach *all* the entities who participated in creating these blocks and obtain their private signing key in order to form the legitimate signatures.

Denial-of-Service Attack. The DoS attack is one of the most commonly observed cyber attacks. The attacker aims at making the system resource unavailable to the legitimate entities either temporarily or indefinitely, typically by flooding the system with a large amount of requests. In SecBITS, as all data and actions are transmitted in the form of a transaction, the attacker could launch a DoS attack by submitting a large number of transactions to the system. To prevent such an attack, we introduce an additional step for generating a valid transaction: one needs to solve a *client puzzle* and embeds the answer into the transaction for validation.

Client puzzle is an approach to increase the cost of a client to carry out certain actions in order to obtain services from the server. Generally, a client puzzle includes puzzle generation, puzzle solving by the client (requires client's effort) and puzzle answer verification by the server (typically easy). In SecBITS, we propose a puzzle that is similar to the "proof-of-work" consensus used in Bitcoin mining process: for the generation of each valid transaction, the submitter needs to guess a random value r such that the hash of r combined with the transaction content tc should satisfy a pre-defined bound (also called *difficulty level*).

Further, this bound is a function with respect to the number of submitted transactions n for a fixed period of time t, i.e., the system will adjust the difficulty level in guessing r. As the only way to produce r is by random guessing, with the increased number of transactions submitted, the number of guesses to obtain a suitable r will drastically increase, and for a DoS attack, this will occur significant computational overhead for the attacker. One could define a suitable client puzzle, set the difficulty based on the system requirement and the capability of an attacker. The selection of a suitable puzzle is out of the scope of this paper.

Rogue Sensor. Sensors located at the data input layer are one of the most vulnerable points that are subjected to security breaches. An attacker may well be interested in aggregating her resources to compromise a single RSU and sending malicious data to the LC, in order to sabotage the traffic decision made for a specific intersection of interest. SecBITS would help to mitigate such an attack through a set of pre-defined rules embedded in the smart contracts. As mentioned earlier, each reported data is embedded in a transaction. Before this transaction calls the smart contract that makes the decision for a particular traffic condition, the validity of this data needs to be checked against relevant information such as data reported in last epoch, or compare with adjacent traffic intersections. Only if the data is within a reasonable range bounded by such relevance check, it then could be fed into the smart contract for current decision.

With carefully designed logic and smart contracts, it would be extremely challenging for an attacker to launch such an attack. As the entire system is connected, the relevant information could be extracted from the ledger efficiently for cross-validation. To launch a successful attack, simply sending a manipulated data is not enough, but rather one needs to understand the relationship for decision making and subsequently modify a chain of data to fool the system. However, as discussed in the *Record Tampering* section, modifying recorded information is also extremely difficult.

Compromised Logic. The road traffic monitoring and the subsequent decision made is heavily based on the logic implemented in the LC. In the case of the LC is compromised, the attacker may manipulate the embedded *logic* to sabotage the traffic system. Under such an attack, note that the decision is still made based on the *correct* data input, whereas the algorithm itself has been changed. For example, an attacker may change the decision of granting 60 s green light based on 100 vehicles reported to only 40 s, causing the traffic jam.

Traditional ITS might not be able to resolve such an attack as the logic is embedded into each individual LC. With SecBITS, the logic could be implemented as a form of smart contract, each with a unique identifier and stored across the entire network on the nodes. A decision made by an LC needs to be verified by the network by calling the designated smart contract used for such decision before it could be executed. As long as the attacker could not possibly compromise a majority of the entities in the network and change the associated smart contract, such a compromised logic attack would be easily detected and the transaction associated with the decision will be rejected.

5   Experiments

We implemented the RSA and ECDSA digital signature schemes and SHA-2 hash function used in SecBITS, to provide assessment for the computational overhead with a varying security level. The schemes are implemented using Python 2.7 on a Windows machine with Intel Core i7-6700 3.40 GHz CPU and 64 GB RAM.

Figure 4 reflects two types of digital signature schemes with a varying security level. RSA-1024 (represented as DSA-1024 in the figure) has the lowest overhead, takes around 1.6 ms for each signature generation. Next, three ECDSA variants and RSA-2048 have relatively close overhead, take approximately 3.3–4.8 ms for each signature generation respectively. Consider the devices collect and transmit data typically in hundreds of millisecond or even second granularity, the overhead for these schemes are acceptable. The overhead for RSA-3072 observed a sharp increase, takes roughly 16.5 ms for one signing procedure. Although the security level is high, the computational time seems a burden for the system participants. Figure 5 plots the signature verification time. The RSA variants could complete the task within extremely short to almost negligible time, approximately less than 1ms for one verification of all variants. For elliptic curve schemes we observed a 2x−3x blow-up of the computational overhead compare to its signing operation.

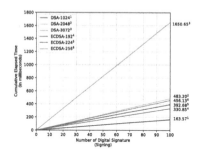

Fig. 4. Signature signing time

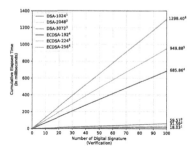

Fig. 5. Signature verification time

We also test the block formation time, i.e., to generate the block identifier by hashing the formed block including header and payload with collected transactions over a period of time. Typically, SHA-256 is sufficient for current security needs, and roughly 680 ms is required if a block contains 100 transactions (Fig. 6).

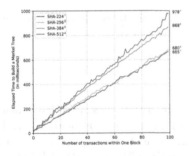

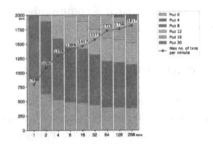

Fig. 6. Block generation time

Fig. 7. Client puzzle solving (Color figure online)

Last, we test our client puzzle idea on a Raspberry Pi (Model 2B). The "X" in Puz X of the legend refers to the number of leading zero bits required in the hash output. We first obtain the number of transactions the device could generate within one minute with no difficulty level as a benchmark, and on average of 800 transactions could be formed (for the compactness of the figure, this value is not included). Subsequently, we set the puzzle level increment threshold to be 320 (i.e., on a 0.4x threshold, 0.4 × 800), that is, for every 320 transactions submitted within the past time epoch, the difficulty level will be increased. The x-axis indicates the varying time epoch, and the y-axis indicates the maximum number of transactions the device could generate within the epoch (red dotted line). One could observe that, even with a geometric growth of the time epoch (i.e., giving an attacker with more time to flood the system), the number of transactions generated only grows (seemingly) linearly, which greatly limits the severity of the attack. The colored bar indicates to which level of difficulty the device could reach within each time epoch (e.g., within four minutes, the device could reach a level of generating 12 leading zero bits for the hash output) (Fig. 7).

6   Conclusion

In this work, we propose SecBITS, a secured blockchain-based intelligent transportation system. We provide detailed system architecture, define transactions and ledger, as well as consensus to ensure a secured global view for the data and information recorded. Further security analysis of four types of attacks and how the proposed system could mitigate such attacks are discussed. Experiments are also conducted to illustrate the feasibility of the proposed solution.

References

1. Zhang, J., Wang, F.-Y., Wang, K., Lin, W.-H., Xu, X., Chen, C.: Data-driven intelligent transportation systems: a survey. IEEE Trans. Intell. Transp. Syst. **12**, 1624–1639 (2011)

2. Kastrinaki, V., Zervakis, M., Kalaitzakis, K.: A survey of video processing techniques for traffic applications. Image Vis. Comput. **21**, 359–381 (2003)

3. Gidel, S., Checchin, P., Blanc, C., Chateau, T., Trassoudaine, L.: Pedestrian detection and tracking in an urban environment using a multilayer laser scanner. IEEE Trans. Intell. Transp. Syst. **11**(3), 579–588 (2010)

4. Seo, T., Kusakabe, T.: Probe vehicle-based traffic state estimation method with spacing information and conservation law. Transp. Res. Part C Emerg. Technol. **59**, 391–403 (2015)

5. Multi-modal intelligent traffic safety system (MMITSS). https://www.its.dot.gov/research_archives/dma/bundle/mmitss_plan.htm

6. Boudguiga, A., et al.: Towards better availability and accountability for IoT updates by means of a blockchain. In: IEEE European Symposium on Security and Privacy Workshops (EuroS&PW). IEEE (2017)

7. Yuan, Y., Wang, F.-Y.: Towards blockchain-based intelligent transportation systems. In: IEEE 19th International Conference on Intelligent Transportation Systems, pp. 2663–2668. IEEE (2016)

8. Leiding, B., Memarmoshrefi, P., Hogrefe, D.: Self-managed and blockchain-based vehicular ad-hoc networks. In: Proceedings of the 2016 ACM International Joint Conference on Pervasive and Ubiquitous Computing: Adjunct, pp. 137–140. ACM (2016)

9. Lei, A., Cruickshank, H., Cao, Y., Asuquo, P., Ogah, C.P.A., Sun, Z.: Blockchain-based dynamic key management for heterogeneous intelligent transportation systems. IEEE IoT J. **4**(6), 1832–1843 (2017)

10. Sharma, P.K., Moon, S.Y., Park, J.H.: Block-VN: a distributed blockchain based vehicular network architecture in smart city. J. Inf. Process. Syst. **13**(1), 84 (2017)

11. Singh, M., Kim, S.: Blockchain based intelligent vehicle data sharing framework. arXiv preprint arXiv:1708.09721 (2017)

Insurance Block: An Insurance Data Security Transaction Authentication Scheme Suitable for Blockchain Environment

Lijun Xiao[1]($\boxtimes$), Yan Cheng[1], Han Deng[1], Shen Xu[2],
and Weidong Xiao[3]

[1] Department of Accounting, Guangzhou College of Technology and Business,
Guangzhou 510850, Guangdong, China
ljxiaoxy@126.com
[2] Taiping Life Insurance Co., Ltd., Guangzhou Central Branch,
Guangzhou 511400, Guangdong, China
[3] School of Software Engineering, Xiamen University of Technology,
Xiamen 361024, Fujian, China

Abstract. In order to solve the problems existing in the sensitive data transaction communication in the insurance industry, such as poor security, high management cost of transaction center, regulatory difficulties and easy data tampering, etc. This paper puts forward a kind of insurance data security transaction authentication scheme based on block chain. This paper proposed a insurance data security transaction authentication scheme based on block chain. With the characteristics of insurance distributed authorization management, the data exchange center is reliable, safe and efficient operation. The scheme can share books, design and implement consensus mechanism of insurance data, intelligent contract and special chain storage structure, as well as multi-party co-storage of data and decentralization of business. Experimental results show that, the block chain insurance data security authentication scheme in this paper has high security and practicability.

Keywords: Blockchain · Insurance data · Consensus mechanism · Smart contracts · Sharing management

1 Introduction

With the rapid development of Internet technology, blockchain technology, as an integrated application of distributed data storage, point-to-point transmission, consensus mechanism, encryption algorithm and other technologies, has been extended to the Internet of things, intelligent manufacturing, supply chain management, digital asset trading and other fields in recent years. For example, in the financial sector, NASDAQ has established a private equity exchange based on blockchain as early as 2015. However, illegal elements use these trading networks to conduct data tampering, theft and online fraud, which has become the mainstream criminal means in blockchain [1–3]. In order to solve the trust problem between communication and transaction parties in various network services, major enterprises and institutions have begun to

© Springer Nature Switzerland AG 2019
M. Qiu (Ed.): SmartBlock 2019, LNCS 11911, pp. 120–129, 2019.
https://doi.org/10.1007/978-3-030-34083-4_12

conduct authentication research on the identity certificate, data storage, asset transaction and currency transfer of blockchain network users. With the expansion of insurance service scenarios and the complexity of operational processes, in many cases, the establishment of third-party central institutions will not only greatly increase the cost of data processing and transaction, but also result in program redundancy and reduced service quality.

In the traditional financial and insurance field, the authentication of user credit information is often complicated, which requires multiple data of users. At the same time, most insurance companies are reluctant to share some data that is conducive to the development of the whole ecological industry for fear of the disclosure of business secrets. For example, blacklists for insurance users, etc. There are data barriers between companies. In the future, it is urgent to solve the problems of user data traceability and user data security sharing in the insurance industry. By upgrading the technology, we can comprehensively optimize and improve the operating efficiency of the industry, so as to obtain value-added service benefits. Block chain technology, as an emerging financial technology, has received extensive attention. Blockchain, with its advantages of third-party removal, non-tampering and auditability, has attracted more attentions in many fields, including the equity trading market, education and the Internet of things. The research on the insurance data identity authentication system based on blockchain will bring the following specific benefits:

1. Through the non-tamperable blockchain data storage, the user's credit data can be stored in the blockchain, and each data can be accurately recorded to the company providing the data, so as to ensure accurate traceability and prevent insurance companies from providing fake situation of the data.
2. The programmable form of intelligent contract will improve the efficiency of the insurance industry. Intelligent contract can automatically deal with many insurance terms and record user credit records, and because it is decentralized, users do not have to worry about insurance company fraud, and solve the trust problem.
3. Decentralized management, if the insurance company establishes an alliance, the traditional form will inevitably require a central insurance company to manage other companies, but using the decentralized nature of the blockchain, decentralized management can be completed. The central node is needed again. For example, when an insurance company is found to provide false information, it can decentralize the vote to decide whether to eliminate the node.
4. The information blockchain is stamped with a time stamp to form non-tamperable data, wherein asymmetric encryption can effectively protect the privacy of user data.

At present, the application of industrial power grid blockchain technology has attracted much attention. The industrial power grid blockchain technology is a reliable data storage technology that involves many power network nodes participating in recording and storing data. Storage decentralization, tamper resistance, and traceability can help solve the above problems people are facing (Fig. 1).

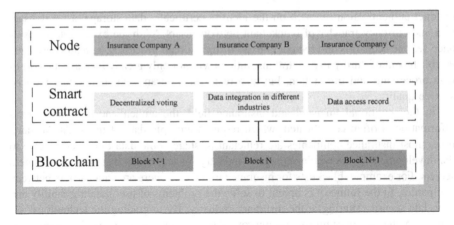

Fig. 1. Application of block chain technology in insurance transaction.

2   Related Work

The research and application of blockchain show the characteristics of alliance, financial level and overall layout. Large stock exchanges in several countries claim to use blockchain technology to increase efficiency and speed up liquidation. In Japan, blockchain technology has been improving since the advent of bitcoin in 2008. Based on the consensus mechanism algorithm, foreign research has proposed a number of new data consensus mechanisms, including proof of stake, delegated proof of stake, ripple, tendermint, etc. These techniques are all to solve the problem caused by Bitcoin's Pow consensus algorithm. The asymmetric encryption used by the blockchain effectively ensures that the user information is not leaked, but other users can still observe the transaction information of the user, including the transaction amount. Therefore, many methods have been proposed to solve these problems, including the zero-knowledge proof algorithm proposed by Zerocoin, which can avoid the leakage of user transaction information but can verify whether the transaction is valid.

The application of current blockchain technology is mainly concentrated in the early experimental and testing phases. Literature [4] designed a multi-center content distribution system based on blockchain, which integrated blockchain into the copyright playback control of digital content. The system replaces the bitcoins circulated in the Bitcoin system with digital content. Similarly, the miners' mining incentives are changed from bitcoins to digital content. The owner of the content in the system issues a permission certificate for the content's demander and sets permissions for the content provided by the user, and can modify the user's rights to play at any time. Block chain records the flow direction of digital content and the content and user's rights. Users play the digital content according to the records in the block chain. Multicentre content distribution system based on block chain changes the traditional CAS and DRM mode, which is more secure than the traditional mode, but makes the key longer and requires longer encryption time. The author in [5] proposes a reputation system based on block chain technology. In this system, the user receives the correct file as a forward transaction. When the user receives the correct file, and sends the transaction containing the credit score, time stamp and the hash value of the received file to the network node. Then the network node encrypts the data with its private key and sends it to the miner for mining. Ensure that users' reputation evaluation is based on real transactions rather than fiction. Therefore, the blockchain stores the credit value of each node in the network transaction.

This paper mainly studies the application of block chain technology in insurance credit investigation, and constructs a credit investigation system based on insurance data of block chain, so as to solve the problems of misleading claims settlement, industry information sharing and insurance fraud. To break through the bottleneck of credit in the insurance industry, it is necessary to solve the problems that have long plagued the development of the insurance industry.

3   Insurance Block Scheme

3.1   Blockchain Sharing Recognition Mechanism

Firstly, the core technology and application principle of insurance blockchain are introduced, and the existing problems in the current power blockchain technology are analyzed. Through the research of intelligent power technology, we will propose a consensus mechanism of data security transmission service suitable for the power blockchain network.

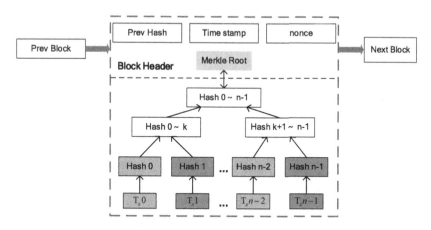

Fig. 2. Insurance block tree data structure.

As shown in Fig. 2, in the blockchain security transmission technology, block is the carrier used for the secure storage of transaction summary information of insurance data, and also the structural unit of the secure storage of insurance data in blockchain [6]. Each block in the figure mainly includes two parts: a block header and a block body. The information in the block header is mainly used to identify the node data of the insurance block, the information summary of the previous block and the position information of the power block data in the whole ledger. Insurance blocks are mainly used to store transaction summary information safely, to verify transaction information with insurance data, and to ensure that transactions can not be tampered with tree information. In different insurance block chains, due to the different rules of network operation mechanism and consensus mechanism, the specific information fields contained in the block head are slightly different. The block header hash value and the block height are not present in the block, but are stored as block metadata in a separate index database for quick retrieval. In addition, there may be information such as difficulty values and random numbers in the block headers of other blockchains. The figure below shows the tree structure of the block header (Fig. 3).

3.2   Chain Storage Structure

The data chain of each insurance block is connected one by one according to the order of generation time to form a chained data storage structure. In the whole chain, the first block is called the creation block, and the height of the block is 0. The height of each block is successively increased by 1, and the hash value of the previous block head is written in the block head.

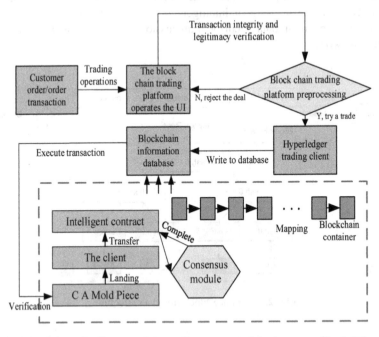

Fig. 3. Schematic diagram of the trading process of the insurance blockchain.

The chained storage structure guarantees irreparable modification of the insurance data stored on the block before the current block. If a malicious node changes the information in a block on the insurance blockchain. Then the Merkle in the block representing the transaction information in all insurance business will change, and the block header hash will change. All the block information after that will change. Therefore, if a malicious node wants to successfully change the transaction information. Only recalculate all subsequent blocks of the changed block and catch up with the progress of the legal blockchain in the network. It is possible to recognize that the chain in which the block is located is forked and submitted to a node in the network. In the context of the powerful data processing capabilities of the current network, it is difficult for a malicious node to recalculate multiple blocks and catch up with the height of the entire network block. Therefore, the irreversible modification of the blockchain data is guaranteed.

3.3   Insurance Data Authentication Based on Blockchain

The nodes include digital authentication (CA) node, billing node sorting service node and endorsement node. The client application represents the physical terminal of the operation. The terminal needs to connect to a billing node or sorting service node to join the blockchain network after communication. The insurance client issues the transaction to the endorsement node, and when the number of endorsements is sufficient, the endorsement node broadcasts the transaction to the sorting service and sorts it, and the main node generates the block. All Peer nodes can be used as accounting nodes, which are responsible for maintaining copies of state data and accounts, and verifying blockchain transactions within sorting service nodes. Some nodes perform trades and endorse the results as endorsement nodes. Endorsement nodes are dynamic roles that can be changed by intelligent contracts. During the process of instantiation, the intelligent contract will set the endorsement policy and specify the validity of the node's transaction endorsement. The CA node is used to receive the registration request from the client. The CA consists of a server and a client component. All operations in the blockchain network authenticate the user's identity. The CA node is optional. In the superbook, Fabric-CA is selected by default, and other third-party CAs can also be used to issue certificates. The data verification process is shown in Fig. 4. When the data is verified, a transaction number bitmap is generated to save each transaction status. The bitmap contains the complete information of the transaction, including the format of the transaction, signature, historical data, and related accounting nodes. Once a discrepancy occurs in the data verification process, the transaction will be marked as invalid transaction, causing the transaction to be cancelled or the transaction to fail. If the transaction is successfully verified, it will be saved to the local ledger and the status database and historical database will be updated. The block generated event is generated afterwards, thereby increasing the block (writing block). In order to improve efficiency, the submission of the state database is batch processing, and the state data of the entire block transaction is submitted at the same time, so that the state data of the entire block does not partially fail partially. At this time, only the recorded book data is inconsistent with the state database, and there is no inconsistency in the state data of the block. The former can be solved by querying the state database mark points.

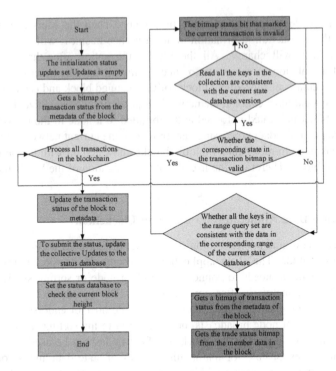

Fig. 4. Block chain based insurance data authentication process diagram.

4 Experimental Results and Analysis

First, the insurance data security storage mechanism in the blockchain network is tested. After confirming the feasibility of the optimization scheme, the insurance data security performance of the blockchain network was tested and compared. Finally, the performance results of the scheme are tested and analyzed according to the data security communication application.

4.1 Network Throughput

According to the detailed function design of the insurance user management module, virtual currency module and sweepstakes module in the insurance application. The corresponding throughput operation was performed on the test machine and the test results were recorded. To test the application's functional implementation and the underlying support of the blockchain.

Suppose a block has a capacity of M bytes and a transaction takes up about a byte. Then it is necessary to satisfy the formula (1), otherwise the block saturation exceeds the capacity limit, so that all transactions cannot be successfully completed.

$$\frac{L\Delta t}{3600T} \leq \frac{1.05 \times 10^6 C}{q}. \tag{1}$$

In addition, the block building time of a block mainly depends on the consensus time. Let's assume that each exchange of messages takes T_1 seconds, and each encryption calculation takes T_2 seconds, then:

$$\Delta t = Kn^2 T_1 + 4Kn^2 T_2 \tag{2}$$

Throughput is the standard to measure the capacity of block chain system to process requests in unit time, and it is also one of the important evaluation indexes to measure the performance of a block chain system. In this paper, the throughput is represented by the number of transactions per second, including copyright registration, copyright transfer and subscription transactions. Throughput v can be expressed as:

$$v = \frac{L_{\Delta t}}{\Delta t}, \tag{3}$$

Where, Δt represents consensus interval. $L_{\Delta t}$ represents the number of transactions contained in a block.

According to the algorithm design, this paper uses Java language to implement the algorithm. Block chain network was built based on insurance data, and throughput was used as an evaluation index to compare with multiple block chain platforms. As shown in Fig. 5, compared with the scheme in literature [7], the data transaction throughput of the insurance block chain network in this paper has a higher capacity.

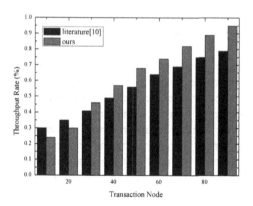

Fig. 5. Schematic diagram of blockchain network throughput comparison.

4.2 Insurance Data Authentication Overhead

During this performance test, Android Studio was used as the test tool. Android Studio is an Android integrated development tool for PC, and can perform basic performance tests on Android applications on PC.

In the process of testing the insurance data of blockchain, this paper adopts the forged attack method to test the data in the process of insurance transaction. The test was first run on a PC to Android Studio. Experimental data and interface display results are shown in Fig. 6. In an insurance application, for example, Gervails' bitinas-simulator simulates the number of block nodes in an insurance blockchain to test the efficiency of anonymizing insurance data. Figure 6 shows the comparison chart of insurance data authentication time of blockchain network. With the increase of tree level number and insurance data capacity, the algorithm in this paper has a better authentication time overhead performance advantage compared with the method in literature [7].

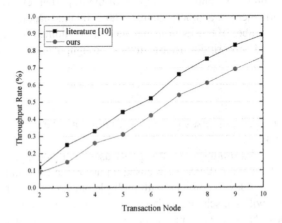

Fig. 6. Comparison of authentication time overhead in the insurance blockchain.

5   Conclusions and Prospect

Aiming at the problems of insurance data transaction scheduling and authentication management on the insurance blockchain. This paper designs a data transaction authentication method based on insurance blockchain technology. This method sets the transaction type of insurance data by designing the mechanism of insurance data transaction security. After completing the registration and authentication process of member management nodes, the authentication of real-time blockchain network insurance data can be achieved by modifying the node configuration file in the process of verifying the normal service of the existing nodes and rebuilding the broadcasting module within the blockchain network. In order to reduce the communication burden of consensus in the authentication process, the purpose of simplifying the consensus process and improving the consensus authentication of insurance data is achieved. This is despite the technical challenges of the certification task. However, insurance blockchain technology has received more and more attention and input from scholars and industry insiders. In the future, the research process will be more smooth, and the above problems and other difficulties encountered in the progress of the application of blockchain will be gradually solved.

References

1. Liang, W., Long, J., Chen, X., Li, K.C.: TBRS: a trust based recommendation scheme for complex CPS network. Future Gener. Comput. Syst. **192**, 383–398 (2018)
2. Gai, K., Wu, Y., Zhu, L., Qiu, M., Shen, M.: Privacy-preserving energy trading using consortium blockchain in smart grid. IEEE Trans. Ind. Inform. **15**(6), 3548–3558 (2019)
3. Liang, W., Tang, M., Long, J., Peng, X., Xu, J., Li, K.C.: A secure fabric blockchain-based data transmission technique for industrial Internet-of-Things. IEEE Trans. Ind. Inform. **15**(6), 3582–3592 (2019)
4. Androulaki, E., et al.: Hyperledger fabric: a distributed operating system for permissioned blockchains. In: Proceedings of the Thirteenth EuroSys Conference 2018, p. 30. ACM (2018)
5. Kishigami, J., Fujimura, J., Watanabe, S., Nakadaira, H., Akutsu, A.: The blockchain-based digital content distribution system. In: IEEE Fifth International Conference on Big Data and Cloud Computing 2015, pp. 187–190. IEEE (2015)
6. Do, H.G., Ng, W.K.: Blockchain-based system for secure data storage with private keyword search. In: IEEE World Congress on Services 2017, SERVICES, pp. 90–93. IEEE (2017)
7. Dubovitskaya, A., Xu, Z., Ryu, S., Schumacher, M., Wang, F.: Secure and trustable electronic medical records sharing using blockchain. In: AMIA Annual Symposium Proceedings 2017, pp. 650–659 (2018)

Price Prediction of Cryptocurrency: An Empirical Study

Liuqing Yang[1], Xiao-Yang Liu[1(✉)], Xinyi Li[1], and Yinchuan Li[1,2]

[1] Columbia University, New York, USA
{ly2335,xl2427,xl2717,yl3923}@columbia.edu
[2] Beijing Institute of Technology, Beijing, China

Abstract. Cryptocurrency has high volatility in market price since its inception. Existing works have explored different models to predict cryptocurrency prices. However, the accuracy is not satisfactory. In this paper, we conduct empirical study on the price forecasting. Firstly, we quantify the entropy and the conditional entropy of cryptocurrencies and stocks, respectively, and find that cryptocurrencies are more difficult to predict than stocks. Secondly, we evaluate various perspectives, including Twitter volume, Twitter sentiment and CNN-LSTM price prediction. Empirical results demonstrated the randomness in price validity, thus no single method is robust enough for cryptocurrency price prediction.

Keywords: Cryptocurrency · Block chain · Price prediction · LSTM

1 Introduction

In the past decade, the cryptocurrency market has skyrocketed from zero to an estimated $300 billion. More than 3,000 cryptocurrencies have been launched. Cryptocurrency prices have much higher volatility, compared with the stocks. Bitcoin alone has fluctuations that ranged from $20,000 to less than $3000, with daily changes of 10%–25%. Therefore, the price prediction of cryptocurrency is fundamentally important for investors.

Many factors contribute the instability of Bitcoin price, such as hash rate of the Bitcoin mining process, the correlation between cryptocurrency and global financial market, and public awareness [2]. In order to reduce investment risks, there are a variety of models currently researched to predict the price including social signal [1], deep reinforcement learning [4], regression [5] and so on.

Cryptocurrency has high volatility in market price since its inception. Existing works have explored different models to predict cryptocurrency prices. However, the prediction accuracy is not satisfactory. In this paper, we conduct empirical analysis on the price forecasting. Firstly, we quantify the entropy and the conditional entropy of cryptocurrencies and stocks, respectively, and find that cryptocurrencies are more difficult to predict than stocks. Secondly, we evaluate various perspectives, including Twitter volume, Twitter sentiment and LSTM price prediction. Empirical analysis results demonstrated the randomness in price

© Springer Nature Switzerland AG 2019
M. Qiu (Ed.): SmartBlock 2019, LNCS 11911, pp. 130–139, 2019.
https://doi.org/10.1007/978-3-030-34083-4_13

validity, thus no single method is robust enough for cryptocurrency price prediction (Fig. 1).

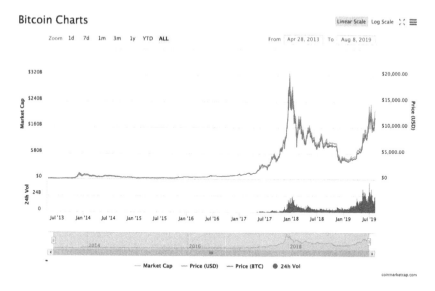

Fig. 1. Bitcoin price chart from its beginning to present (from coinmarketcap.com).

2   Empirical Characterization pf Price Predictability

2.1   Entropy and Conditional Entropy

In information theory [12], the conditional entropy quantifies the amount of uncertainty of a random variable given that the the random variable at a previous time stamp is known.

Temporal Entropy is defined as the entropy of a state sequence. Let Q denote the total number of states, σ_k denote the occurrence frequency of the k-th state, we have the probability P_k and the entropy $H(S)$ as follows

$$P_k = \lim_{T \to \infty} \frac{\sigma_k}{T} \, , \qquad H(S_i) = -\sum_{k=0}^{Q-1} P_k \cdot \log P_k. \tag{1}$$

Temporal Conditional Entropy [12] is defined as the entropy of $S_{i,t}$ when each element's immediately previous state S_{t-1} is known, computed as:

$$H(S_t | S_{t-1}) = H(S_t, S_{t-1}) - H(S_{t-1}), \tag{2}$$

where $H(S_t, S_{t-1})$ is the joint entropy of two consecutive states (S_t, S_{t-1}). Then, we have the temporal entropy and conditional entropy for n cryptocurrencies or stocks, and the CDFs (cumulative distribution function) accordingly.

2.2   Predictability of Cryptocurrencies Vs Stocks

In probability theory and statistics, the cumulative distribution function (CDF) of a real-valued random variable X, or just distribution function of X, evaluated at X, is the probability that X will take a value less than or equal to X.

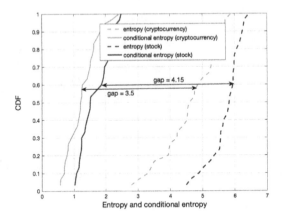

Fig. 2. Gap between entropy and conditional entropy.

As shown in Fig. 2, we plot the CDF for the conditional entropy and entropy of top 30 cryptocurrencies and of 30 stocks in the Dow Jones, respectively. Comparison of the gap shows that cryptocurrencies is much smaller than that for stocks, indicating that the cryptocurrency price is harder to predict.

3   Different Perspectives

3.1   Twitter Volume Analysis

Unlike traditional currencies, there is no government to control the price value of cryptocurrencies, and their values are purely dependent on public belief. Considered one of the most widely used, public, social platforms, Twitter is an ideal data resource that reflects the public's attitude towards cryptocurrency. To a certain degree, the volume of tweets from one specific time period depicts the amount of attention paid to a single topic, at a particular time.

3.2   Twitter Sentiment Analysis

It is well known that the value of Bitcoin is dependent on public belief. In order to conduct further research, we investigate the content of these tweets and analyze the public's attitude towards cryptocurrency. The content of the tweets provide a more detailed information about the tweets themselves. Analyzing the sentiment behind tweets can be used to determine whether they are negative or positive. Through analysis of a large number of tweets, a general consensus relating to the public's attitude could be determined. To analyze this process, we use Natural Language Processing.

1. Bitcoin ATMs Continue to Spread Across the Globe – Bitcoin News http://j.mp/2FjlxPv
2. Russia to buy billions of dollars worth of bitcoin in February. http://Otcbid.com # bitcoin

bitcoin	atm	continue	spread	across	globe	bitcoin	news	http
russia	buy	billion	dollar	worth	bitcoin	february	http	bitcoin

NLTK sentiment analysis

	megative	neutral	positive	compound
tweet 1	0	1	0	0
tweet 2	0	0.921	0.079	0.2263

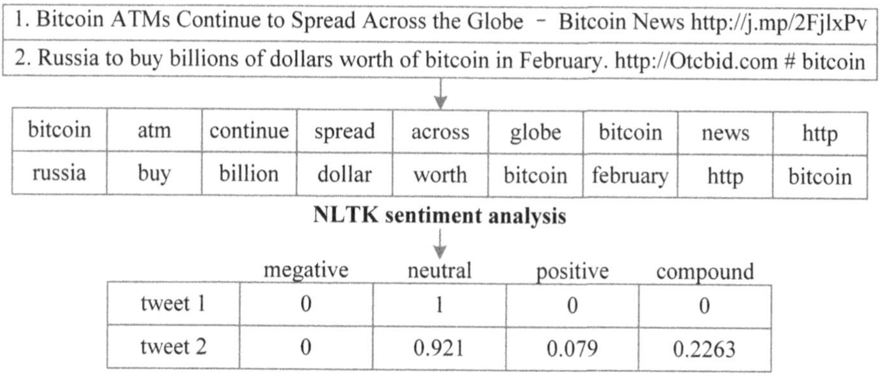

Fig. 3. Preprocessing of tweets.

Natural Language Processing attempts to interact and understand text or speech using computer programs, instead of human beings. NTLK stands for Natural Language Toolkit (NLTK), and it contains packages to create appropriate responses to various scenarios.

NLTK Processing Procedure. After processing the collected tweets in 2019, we apply nature language processing methods. Figure 3 illustrates the specific process of the NLTK sentiment analysis. First, it filters all the meaningless words like web URLs, which might interfere with the result. As shown in the sentences at the top and bottom, using this natural language analysis, it separates each sentence word by word, and then employs an algorithm to figure out which ones are negative, which are neutral, and which are positive. It also takes a combination of words into consideration. Finally, each sentence get assigned with a score simply by Sentiment Intensity Analyzer.

3.3   Technical Analysis Based on Deep Learning

The goal of this analysis is to establish a value for the cryptocurrency, that would factor in all the underlying factors. Since this involves the use of forward-looking expectations, this methodology is utilized to design a valuation, based on backward-looking and forward-looking information. Corresponding to Fig. 4, this differs from sentiment analysis, since technical analysis obtains cryptocurrency's price and volume as the only inputs.

The long short-term memory (LSTM) neural network [3], compared with a regular neutral network model, has several advanced features. When saving the history data, it uses a forgetting gate to filter the meaningless data. When using the history data to boost the current prediction, it uses a selection gate to pick only the most valuable data. So, even data that is far from the current loop will influence the result. CNN LSTM structures involves using convolution layer for feature extraction into LSTM for sequtial prediction. We design a model that takes advantages of LSTM, RNN and CNN-sliding window model for cryptocurrency price prediction.

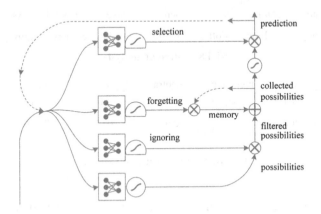

Fig. 4. Overview of the LSTM neural network.

LSTM Network. The LSTM network in Fig. 4 consists of four gates: input gate, ignoring gate, forgetting gate and selection gate. Each gate contains its own neutral network and squashing process. The memory part in the middle takes copy of current prediction into next timestamp, and then forgetting gate direct necessary information to be cumulatively remembered.

- Input gate controls the information from a new input to the memory cell

$$i_t = \sigma(W_i \times [h_{t-1}, \mathcal{X}_t^{\text{train}}] + b_i), \tag{3}$$

$$\hat{c}_t = \tanh(W_c \times [h_{t-1}, \mathcal{X}_t^{\text{train}}] + b_c), \tag{4}$$

where h_{t-1} is the hidden state at the time step $t-1$; i_t is the output of the input gate layer at the time step t; $\hat{c}_t$ is the candidate value to be added to the output at the time step t; b_i and b_c are biases of the input gate layer and the candidate value computation, respectively; W_i and W_c are weights of the input gate and the candidate value computation, respectively; and sigmoid $\sigma(x) = 1/(1 + e^{-x})$ is a pointwise nonlinear activation function.
- Ignoring gate is an intention mechanism that prevents memory content from being disturbed by unrelated input.
- Forgetting gate controls the limit up to which a value is saved in the memory

$$f_t = \sigma(W_f \times [h_{t-1}, \mathcal{X}_t^{\text{train}}] + b_f), \tag{5}$$

where f_t is the forgetting state at the time step t, W_f is the weight of forgetting gate; and b_f is the bias of forgetting gate.

– Selection gate controls the information output from the memory cell

$$c_t = f_t \times c_{t-1} + i_t \times \hat{c}_t, \tag{6}$$
$$o_t = \sigma(W_o \times [h_{t-1}, \mathcal{X}_t^{\text{train}}] + b_o), \tag{7}$$
$$h_t = o_t \times \tanh(c_t), \tag{8}$$

where new cell states c_t are calculated based on the results of the previous two steps; o_t is the selected output at the time step t; W_o is the weight of the selection gate; and b_o is the bias of the selection gate.

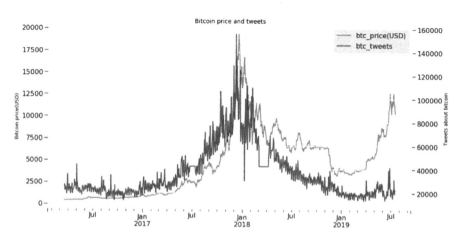

Fig. 5. BTC price vs Twitter volume.

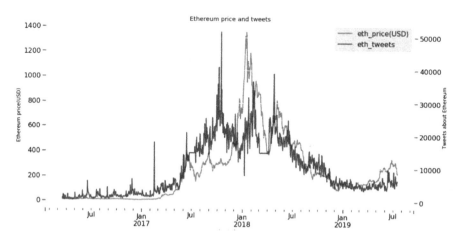

Fig. 6. ETH price vs Twitter volume.

Data Preprocessing. More accurately, the price prediction we performed is to predict whether the price will increase or decrease on the next day. From the perspective of a buyer, if the price goes up, it is reasonable to buy. If the price goes down, it is better to not buy. We can look at the accuracy of trend prediction in this case.

As shown in Table 1, it is a simple example of the data after processing. Since day 1 and day 3 had a lower price than that on the next day, they were marked as 1, which indicates a "buy" option. Day 2 had a higher price than the price for the next day, and was marked as 0, which indicates a "not buy" option.

Table 1. Preprocessing

Date	Volume	Price	Buy (1) or Sell (0)
1	1000	100	1
2	1000	102	0
3	1000	99	1
4	1000	100	0

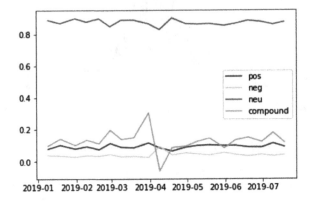

Fig. 7. NLTK results.

4 Empirical Study

4.1 Twitter Volume Analysis

Bitcoin (BTC) Results. It can be seen from Fig. 5 that the ETC price is almost consistent with the volume of tweets. Except for the ETC price peak in January 2018, and the peak of tweets at the end of 2017, both the curves are basically the same for other time periods. As for the relationship between the BTC price and tweets volume, we can clearly see that the trend of curve fluctuation is consistent, except for the current year, which indicates a strong correlation.

Ethereum (ETH) Results. It can be seen from Fig. 6 that the ETH price is almost consistent with the volume of tweets, except for the peak time. ETC price peaks in January 2018, and the amount of tweets reach its peak at the end of 2017. In other words, Twitter discussion about Ethereum goes up first before price catchs up with the momentum.

4.2   Twitter Sentiment Analysis

Fig. 8. Wordcloud: positive and negative tweets.

Our NTLK model obtains results as shown in Fig. 7, where the blue line is always over the yellow line, and the compound score is always greater than zero, which indicates that the sentiment score of all the tweets in 2019 has been positive. We can conclude that the public holds a positive attitude towards Bitcoin, and its price will see a rising trend in 2019. The Bitcoin price graph below just confirmed our prediction.

Figure 8 were created using all the words which occur in 2019's tweets. The size of a word represents the frequency of the word's usage in positive and negative directions. The more frequently a word appears, the larger the word's size. In positive tweets, we can see bigger words like Crypto, new, money, good, price etc. Interestingly, among the negative tweets, we can see that "crypto" is the biggest word, as well as other words such as cryptocurrency, mine, new and ban.

4.3   LSTM BTC Results

For each cryptocurrency, the data has been collected from the day it was launched, or from when it began generating some market value. For example, for Bitcoin (BTC), the data has been collected from April 28th, 2013 to the present day. For Ethereum (ETH), it is from August 07th, 2015 to the present day.

We considered two datasets to validate the prediction performance. After processing the data, the entire dataset was used as the first dateset and was divided into two parts where 80% was used as a training set, and the 10% data

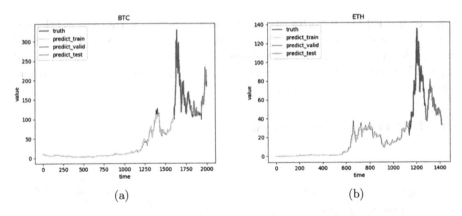

Fig. 9. Prediction result of LSTM based on price only. (Color figure online)

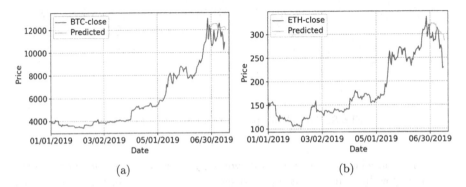

Fig. 10. Prediction result of LSTM based on price, Twitter volume and NLTK results.

was used as a validation set to test the trained model, and final 10% data for testing. The second dataset was the data from January 1st, 2019 to July 15th, 2019 (corresponding to the duration of tweets that we analyzed in Fig. 7) and was divided into two parts where 85% was used as a training set, and the rest for testing. The second dataset is used to validate the prediction performance based on the price, Twitter volume (shown in Figs. 5 and 6) and NLTK results (shown in Fig. 7), i.e., we input cryptocurrency price, Twitter volume and NLTK results into LSTM network together to obtain the predicted price.

We can see the result of BTC in Fig. 9(a). Both for the validation part and for testing part, the fitting of the graph is highly accurate. Prediction result of ETH is shown in Fig. 9(b). After the training, we have validation and testing results compared with the actual performance. The overlapping of the colored lines indicates the robustness of this method.

At last, Figs. 10(a) and (b) present the predicted results of LSTM based on price, Twitter volume and NLTK results for BTC and ETH, respectively. The prediction accuracy of them are respectively 92.26% and 91.84%. We can see that the Twitter volume and NLTK results can help predict the cryptocurrencies.

5   Conclusions

The entropy characterization quantitatively show the high difficulty for cryptocurrency price prediction. Then we demonstrate an empirical analysis to predict the prices of cryptocurrencies. The methods used are volume and content analysis of Twitter, and NLTK implementation for social sentiments, as well as LSTM model for direct price prediction. We evaluate these models on two cryptocurrencies, where each method has solid result that facilitates reliability and stability for prediction. Our empirical analysis may be used for cryptocurrency investment [11].

References

1. Garcia, D., Schweitzer, F.: Social signals and algorithmic trading of Bitcoin. Royal Soc. Open Sci. **2**(9), 150288 (2015)
2. Kristoufek, L.: What are the main Drivers of the Bitcoin Price? Evidence from Wavelet Cohernce Analysis (2015)
3. Greff, K., Srivastava, R.K., Koutník, J., Steunebrink, B.R., Schmidhuber, J.: LSTM: a search space odyssey. IEEE Trans. Neural Networks Learn. Syst. **28**(10), 2222–2232 (2016)
4. Jiang, Z., Liang, J.: September. Cryptocurrency portfolio management with deep reinforcement learning. In: IEEE Intelligent Systems Conference (IntelliSys), pp. 905–913 (2017)
5. Songmuang, K.: The forecasting of cryptocurrency price by correlation and regression analysis. Kasem Bundit J. **19**(May–June), 287–296 (2018)
6. Colianni, S., Rosales, S., Signorotti, M.: Algorithmic trading of cryptocurrency based on Twitter sentiment analysis. CS229 Project, 1–5
7. Sasank Pagolu, V., Reddy, K.N., Panda, G., Majhi, B.: Sentiment analysis of Twitter data for predicting stock market movements. In: SCOPES (2016)
8. Li, X., Li, Y., Liu, X.-Y., Wang, D.: Risk management via anomaly circumvent: mnemonic deep learning for midterm stock prediction. In: KDD Workshop on Anomaly Detection in Finance (2019)
9. Cryptodatadownload. http://www.cryptodatadownload.com/. Accessed 20 July 2019
10. Coin Market Cap. https://coinmarketcap.com/. Accessed 10 July 2019
11. Xiong, Z., Liu, X.-Y., Zhong, S., Yang, H., Walid, A.: Practical deep reinforcement learning approach for stock trading. In: NeurIPS Workshop on Challenges and Opportunities for AI in Financial Services: the Impact of Fairness, Explainability, Accuracy, and Privacy (2018)
12. Cover, T.M., Thomas, J.A.: Elements of Information Theory. Wiley, Hoboken (2012)

Author Index

Printed in the United States
By Bookmasters